To Be The Best

Reflections of a Champion

To the Lord, who loaned me the ability that I have, and also to my entire family, who have given me the love and encouragement that a father and husband needs.

Other books by Gary Player:

Golf Begins at Fifty
124 Golf Lessons
World Golfer
Gary Player's Golf Secrets
Positive Golf
395 Golf Lessons
Gary Player on Fitness and Success
Gary Player's Golf Book for Young People
Grand Slam Golf

To Be The Best

Reflections of a Champion

Gary Player
with Michael McDonnell

Sidgwick & Jackson Limited
London

First published in Great Britain in 1991 by Sidgwick & Jackson
Limited

ISBN 0–283–06007–7

Photoset by Parker Typesetting Service, Leicester
Printed by
Butler & Tanner Ltd, Frome and London
for Sidgwick & Jackson Limited
Cavaye Place
London SW10 9PG

Contents

Foreword
by Arnold Palmer

Gary Player's accomplishments in golf and life rival the achievements of any person who has ever played the game. The record is there for all to see and admire. Gary scored some 140 victories in all parts of the world in a career spanning nearly forty years, the most important of which are his nine in golf's major championships. As the winner of all four majors – three Masters and British Opens, two PGAs and the 1966 US Open – Gary occupies a place in the game's history shared only with Jack Nicklaus, Ben Hogan and Gene Sarazen. He has continued as a dominant player in senior golf with eighteen wins in his first five years after passing the fifty mark, many of them in the senior majors.

But, to me, the obstacles that Gary Player overcame in the formative years of his career are what made his great success so remarkable and admirable. He was a youngster of small stature in a family of modest means. His mother had died when he was just eight. As he learned to play the game in his native South Africa, a country remote from the important events and tours of the time in the United States, he nevertheless aspired to a career as an international tournament player. Against that background, he was determined to succeed and he was aggressive about it in the competitive meaning of the word. Knowing that he needed strength and stamina to complete successfully on the world tours, Gary worked hard on his physical conditioning, something that concerned few golfers of the time. It served him well as, with little money in his pocket, he began to make those long trips from South Africa, spending not hours but days on those old propeller-driven airplanes en route to the tournaments. He was really a pioneer, learning to play under all sorts of adverse conditions, in terms of the courses and the weather, without always having the best equipment – clubs, shoes, clothing. What today's players have was unheard of in those days.

Gary was determined to be a winner and developed his physical strength so that he could hit the ball far enough to be a constant threat in any championship on the longest of courses. Yet, he also had the ability to improvise and win on courses that were extremely narrow. He learned to play and win under all kinds of conditions. He is a perfect example for any young player of how to play the game and use your ability and physical being to become successful, without having the advantages of money and modern conveniences.

I remember when Gary first came to America to play in 1957. We had all heard about this 21-year-old from South Africa who had played well in Britain and was going to set all kinds of records on our Tour. I had listened to such things about other newcomers, who didn't live up to their billings, so, like others, I was a bit sceptical. On the other hand, I had heard from people whose judgment I respected that Gary had a chance to be a very fine player. It didn't take him long at all to prove them correct. We hit it off pretty well when we got to know each other, and by the early 1960s had become good friends.

This, in turn, led to our mutual association with Mark McCormack, who has managed our business affairs ever since. In 1959, as my success on the PGA Tour was growing, so were my activities and offers of work beyond the tournaments, complicating my life and threatening to interfere with the golf itself. Mark had been doing some work for several of us players. I liked what I saw, asked him to represent me exclusively and we struck a deal with a handshake – nothing more. It wasn't a one-client arrangement for very long. Gary began to experience the same sort of off-course distractions that I had. He came to me in 1960 and asked if I would mind if Mark McCormack represented him, too. My deal with Mark was that he could not manage anybody else, but I told him he could handle Gary. So, Gary became the second client and the growth of McCormack's International Management Group was on its way.

Having the same management, Gary and I were booked for many exhibitions together and played as a team against all comers in a television series called 'Challenge Golf' for several years. We had a tremendous record on that show, losing very few matches, and it really cemented our friendship. We maintained an excellent relationship throughout all of those matches. I'm not sure that many people could do that! Jack Nicklaus, who became Mark's third client, joined us in a subsequent TV show, 'Big Three Golf'.

Memorable, too, was the time in 1962 when I took my family, including my parents, to South Africa to visit the Players and their country while Gary and I were playing a series of exhibitions there. Our family and personal friendship has continued to this day and I am proud of it.

CHAPTER 1
'I Know You Can Hear Me . . .'

I was eight years old when they told me my mother had died. I had been taken to visit her in the Kensington Sanatorium and I knew she was in intense pain. My father asked me to wait outside the door so that I would not see her suffering. She had cancer and underwent a series of operations but there was to be no miracle cure. The most important person in my life just simply slipped away and there was nothing I could do to help her.

She died almost fifty years ago but I have to admit she has never really left me. Even now I can still remember her vividly. I remember her voice; the things she told me. I can see every line and characteristic of her face. And she has remained the most important influence on my life. All that I am and all that I have become is in some way a tribute to her. It has been a means for me, as it were, to settle some unfathomable debt.

But there is more to it than that. Throughout my adult life, I have had the same dream over and over. It happens about twice a year and never changes in any detail; and I always wake up in tears. In my dream I see my mother. I call her and try to tell her what I have achieved; how successful I have been and how proud she can be of me. But she cannot hear me. I implore her to listen, but it is as though she is deaf. She doesn't pay attention. I begin to cry in frustration and when I wake up, though I know it has only been a dream, the tears are real. Perhaps a psychoanalyst would reveal the hidden meaning of it all. What I know is that for all my success, fame, fortune, my own delightful children and grandchildren, the burning regret is that she never saw what I had made of myself.

My only personal souvenir is a sketch of her with my father which I keep in my room. But the truth is that I don't even need that reminder because she is as clear in my mind as if she had just slipped out of the house for a moment. She was a gentle woman who combined love with discipline. She would kneel by my bedside every night while I said my prayers. And she constantly insisted on correct manners and behaviour.

'Put your tie on properly, my boy!'
'You didn't stand up when Auntie Roma came into the room!'
'Don't stretch across the table!'
'And don't sit down until you come and put my chair in for me!'
They were to be lessons well learned no matter how rigorous they
seemed to be at the time. I have acted the same way with my own
children and passed on her values to them.

Looking back, I now believe that the championship career of Gary
Player began with that trauma in my life: it was the moment my
personal case-hardening started, even though I was too young to
know it. The reason and purpose of all that followed can be traced
back to my mother's untimely death. That loss was to breed an
independence, a toughness of spirit, and an awareness of adversity
and discipline that have never left me.

At that early age I lived a solitary life. My father worked down the
gold mines and left home before dawn. I would awake in an empty
house, make my own breakfast, then travel for almost two hours
across Johannesburg to school. When I came home in the evening the
darkened house would still be empty and until I plucked up courage
to go in alone I would sit in a bus shelter across the street and wait for
my dad or sister to come home. Sometimes a neighbour, Lourens
Pretorius, would notice me and invite me into his house.

By the time I was nine I had lost my fear of being alone. My
personal routine never changed. I would enter my room, take off my
shoes and remove my socks and tuck them into the right shoe. To this
day, I still follow the same ritual in the locker-room after golf or even
if I change to go for a swim. I would then take off the school uniform
– green blazer, grey trousers, white shirt and the green and white tie –
hang them neatly over a chair and get into my old clothes. Even at
that young age I imposed on myself the kind of strict discipline most
other youngsters observed sullenly by complying with frequently
repeated parental orders. But there was nobody to order me around.
Of course, the other reason for this inflexible routine was that the
same shirt and socks had to see me through the week. No fresh daily
change of clothing in those days.

It was therefore a solitary personal existence, even though at King
Edward VII School I was an outgoing personality, not much of a
scholar but excellent at most sports and regarded as a popular (if, at
times, cocky) chap.

In a very real sense, my adult life and professional career reflected
those beginnings. In fact, that childhood prepared me for the kind of

life I was destined to lead as an international sportsman roaming the world. Looking back, I find myself reflecting on the words of Sir Winston Churchill when, in another context, he said: 'I felt as if I were walking with destiny, and that all my past life had been but a preparation for this hour ...'

I am convinced that the routine of personal discipline I have observed since boyhood has been the real reason I have endured as a champion and a competitor. It has taken various forms, not least of which is the physical fitness routine I follow every day. There is, however, a value more important, perhaps, than the feeling of well-being this ritual brings. It is the complete control and mental discipline to follow these punishing exercises, even when the body screams out 'stop'. Even now, I will not go to bed at night without doing my exercises, no matter how late I get back to my room. Moreover, I sometimes like to surprise my body. Instead of doing a fixed regular quota of sit-ups, I may suddenly double the number; and almost every day I force myself to hit practice shots, even when I am not competing. Just occasionally the thought strikes me: 'Gary, after all you have achieved, what on earth are you doing all this for now?' But the mood soon passes. I refuse to let it linger. What I have done is to tighten the personal control and strength that almost certainly marks the difference between winning and losing in moments of pressure. Globe-trotting golf is a solitary existence, no matter how well-known and widely acclaimed I might be. I travel a lot on my own. I estimate I have flown 7 million miles in my career. For most of that time I have lived alone in motel rooms. I eat alone. I practise alone. And even though there may be thousands of people watching a tournament, I am by myself out there. It is just me against the rest.

That truly was the spirit that stirred within me in those early years. I had learned from my mother's death the most valuable lesson about life – and, curiously enough, about golf itself. It had happened and there was nothing I could do to change it. The ball just had to be played as it lay. There was no point in protesting about bad luck or cursing misfortune or demanding why it had happened to me. The only task was to make the best of what was left and to get on with it.

It is in the nature of this game that a player has to be introspective. He must be honest with himself. He must recognize his strengths and weaknesses no matter what he admits to the outside world, because when the front door closes, he is alone with himself. What I have learned about myself is that I am animal when it comes to achievement and wanting success. There is never enough success for me. I cannot attain enough. And I don't know the reason for this need. Even as I get closer to sixty, the desire is still there. My son Wayne is more naturally talented than I but he doesn't have the same desire in professional golf. I don't love him any the less because of it. But he says he wants to enjoy his life as well as play golf; my enjoyment always came from winning and the sense of achievement it brought. I was once having dinner with the late President Eisenhower and we were talking about war. He said, 'You fight a war to win. You don't prolong it.' In other words, you get in and do the job properly or else get out. There are no half-measures.

We all have different ideas of the nature of success. Mine is fairly precise. The best score. The top prize. The riches. But then I think about my father Harry. He worked down the gold mines for a hundred pounds a month. Even so, he had great success. He was a giant of man, literally, at 6ft 1in (I take after my diminutive mother). He had a loud and hearty laugh. He spoke several black languages. Everybody loved him. He enjoyed his golf at the weekend. He was truly a fulfilled man. That has to be success. He was a great influence on my life and probably my closest friend until he died in 1977.

When I was at school I told him I intended to be the best golfer in the world. I don't think he was too convinced. But he said to me: 'If you really believe that, then you've got to take elocution lessons at school because it's important to speak well.' And so, after school and before I made that two-hour journey home, I would have elocution lessons. My teacher was a Mrs Henning and she would declare: 'Stand up and speak up, Player! You are not pronouncing your words correctly. Don't be shy!'

I can be thankful that my father was around to see me become a champion. I made him retire and I took him all over the world. He loved golf and was devoted to me. One year at Royal Birkdale I spent four hours on the practice tee in the rain working on my swing during the Open championship. He lay on the ground in his big overcoat and old hat for all that time, and as I practised, he ignored the rain but said: 'I can hear the shots are good, son. Like a sheet being torn. Zip! Zip! Zip!' Sometimes I would touch his ear playfully and he'd smile.

In later life, we were more like pals. I was at his bedside when he died. He was seventy-eight and the years of working in the mine had taken their toll. He had dust in his lungs, a complaint known as phthisis that is an occupational hazard for those who work in the mines. Only one kidney functioned, he had ulcers and sugar diabetes. I remember thinking what a sacrifice he had made, working 10,000 feet down in the gold mine for fourteen hours a day. I was once at the mine when he came to the surface and his boots were filled with water. I thought there had been a flood but it was his own perspiration. There was no air-conditioning at that depth. Here, now, was this larger-than-life man on the brink of death. I remembered how he had gone into debt to get me started in professional golf when he secured an overdraft from the bank to send me on my first trip in Britain in 1955. He only told me this many years later.

Now, it was almost over. He lay in bed. His eyes were open but he was losing touch. He couldn't speak. He kept shaking his head from side to side. The shaking got worse. It was as though he knew he was going to die and he was fighting it. I said softly: 'Dad, I know you can hear me. You are looking at me. You have been a fantastic father. I just want you to know that. If you can hear me, just move your mouth. I know you can't talk. Just say that you love me.' The lips moved. There was a faint whisper. Yet it was unmistakable: 'Love . . . you.' He died the next day.

I have tried throughout my life to behave towards my own children as he treated me. Even now I will kiss my grown-up sons as he kissed me. Why should adulthood change the way we treated them as children? When they were young I smacked them if they were naughty, but never in temper. I have never lost my temper with them. We have been separated by my career. I have cried when I had to leave them but they were never out of my thoughts. I still carry letters they have written to me and sometimes I take them out of my briefcase on a plane and re-read them because of the warmth and love they reveal.

My son Marc weighs 200lb, is as strong as a lion and a very aggressive businessman. Yet he wrote to me recently saying: 'You have not only been my father but my friend and my mentor.' I am an emotional man. I cry very easily. And when he was younger Marc would blink back his own tears as we parted, refusing to let go because he felt the family looked to him while I was away.

Even though we were separated by distance we have always remained close as a family. We still follow the Zulu tradition of having an *indaba* – a meeting in which we get together to clear the air. It happens once a year, generally around Christmas when all the family – the six children as well as Vivienne and myself – are at our farm, Blair Atholl, or at the beach house. It is strictly no-holds-barred stuff. I might say to Wayne that I was unhappy at the way he got off a plane unshaven and wearing jeans and sneakers. And he might say: 'Well, dad, you haven't actually been showing much interest in what I've been doing in golf during the last few months.' I may have to swallow my pride and say: 'You're right. I'm sorry.' This is our way of taking stock. It is also the weekly routine we observe on my farms when all the workers get together and have their say. And we have ours too.

Our family *indaba* can last for two hours or more and it can be pretty heavy talk. The talk often turns to whether the children have problems coping with my fame and find life more difficult because of it. Certainly Wayne has had a hard time because he followed me into the same profession. He was once ordered to leave a golf course because he was wearing jeans. He was branded as something of a brat because he threw a club against his bag and growled 'Dammit' when he thinned a ball out of a bunker after hitting a stone. I said: 'My boy, people are watching you like a hawk because you are my son. That's tough. They are trying to get at me through you. People always have more pleasure in criticizing than praising. But you've got to learn to take it. And it's going to make a man of you in the long run. Anyway, let's look the advantages of being the son of a famous father. There are plenty of them.' He had to agree. After all, how many young pros are invited to play by Lee Trevino? And Wayne also had the chance to play with the legendary Jimmy Demaret before he died. These are some of the bonuses he could not ignore.

I have never indulged my children. Jack Nicklaus and I are both proud of our families. But I suspect Jack thinks my ideas are too regimented and strict. Over the years, for example, all my children have known they can come to me to help them out financially; but they also know that I expect it back. More importantly, they insist on that condition too. They would not have it any other way. I sponsor Wayne as a golf professional. We have a contract. As he makes money, so he pays me back. All of my children have shown the kind of independence that fate forced on me all those years ago when my mother died. My daughter Michelle is a prime example. When she gained her business degree I offered to give her a round-the-world ticket. She declined. She wanted to do it on her own, working in a kibbutz in Israel then as a waitress all over the world before coming home to a highly successful job in the fashion industry. I fretted as a parent but I admired that spirit. I recognize it too in my other daughters, Jennifer, Theresa and Amanda, the youngest, as they make their way. It is the freedom and confidence to attempt whatever they desire. That in itself is probably the greatest success of all. It is a priceless legacy, more valuable than any riches.

CHAPTER 2
'It's Never Over Till It's Over'

Looking back, there seems to have been a recurring element of drama in most of my famous victories, as though it were the essential hallmark of the Gary Player style of winning. Even now, I can still re-live those moments when everything hung on my next move. While others plodded, or surged, in skilful manner towards glory, it seemed I would reach the edge of near-disaster, then haul myself back – like a tightrope walker who slips but regains his balance just in time.

Back in 1959 I had to wait two hours to discover whether I was British Open champion. I was convinced I had thrown the title away when it had been firmly within my grasp and I could only wait in anguish to see if any of my rivals at Muirfield could catch me. I went back to my hotel. I had a cold bath. I got dressed. I waited. Harold Henning, a fellow professional, phoned me with news of how the leaders were doing. I went back to Muirfield but could not bear to watch. I paced up and down the drive away from the clubhouse. Finally, George Gibson, then boss of the Professional Golfers' Co-operative Association, persuaded me to come into the building and watch the final moments of the championship from an upstairs room overlooking the last green. From there, I beheld Flory Van Donck and Fred Bullock poised over their birdie putts for the chance to tie. At that moment, I pondered on how I had squandered a glorious day's play at the moment when I almost had a great score in my pocket. It was a lesson I was never to forget: the game is never over until the last putt drops.

On that final day we had played two rounds, as was the custom of the time, and I started in confident mood, even though I was eight strokes behind the leader and there were a dozen other players separating us. In fact on the previous evening I had sat down and analysed their strengths and weaknesses and come to the conclusion I could overtake all of them. I dined with my close friend the late George Blumberg and told him: 'I am going to win it tomorrow. I will go for every shot.' By lunchtime on the final day I was four strokes off the lead and by the afternoon I stood on the last tee needing a four for a 66 which I knew would put me well beyond the reach of the leaders, who still had nine holes to play.

From this position of virtual success I managed to score a double-bogey six down that final stretch and offer the title on a plate to anybody who had the courage to take it. The crisis had started so innocently when I drove down the left-hand side intending to fade the ball off the bunkers and into the fairway; but instead it was trapped. I hacked the ball 100 yards then hit a six-iron approach which only just reached the front edge of the green. Instantly there was a gnawing awareness that this title was slipping away and I sensed a half-formed suspicion of self-doubt about my own inner strength. I took three putts up the hill for my six. People thought I cried as I handed in my card. I felt like it. But they would have been tears of anger, not sorrow, at such a stupid error. Yet mercifully I was to be reprieved by the mistakes of others. Both Flory and Fred missed their putts – and I had won my first major title.

I realized then there were many ways of winning titles other than that classic walk down the last fairway acknowledging the cheering crowds; and indeed, the scenario at Muirfield was not to be the last time I would become champion while, as it were, sitting in the clubhouse. My first US Masters triumph followed a similar pattern as I watched my close friend and rival Arnold Palmer throw away his chance of victory on the last green in 1961.

I have to say that for a time on that final day at Augusta I thought I had the title firmly in my grasp. I was three strokes in the lead when I came to the thirteenth hole, which at the time was unquestionably the best par-five in the world because of the demands it made on judgement, strategy and skill. I drove too far to the right towards the trees, then compounded the error by becoming too impatient. The sensible shot was to take a six iron down the adjacent fourteenth fairway, then put my third on the green almost by the side-door from that right-hand side. But the crowds were slow in moving and I could not wait. I had a title to win. So I decided instead to jab the ball through the trees and back to the fairway. The shot was too strong and the ball ran into the creek.

It cost me a penalty stroke to retrieve the ball and drop clear, and once again I found myself fighting a battle to retain control of my emotions and judgement. I was clearly worried about fluffing my wedge shot back into the creek and in consequence hit the ball too strongly to the back of the green and three-putted for a double-bogey seven. My lead had vanished and though I scrambled over the closing holes, it was Arnold who stood in the middle of the last fairway needing no more than a seven iron to the green and requiring a par-four to make sure of the title. Vivienne and I had gone into the clubhouse to watch the final moments on television as the entire nation, it seemed, waited for their hero to score another inevitable triumph.

As I watched, I was struck once again by the thought of how I had wasted all my good golf of the week by that error of judgement on the long thirteenth. But then I reasoned that success comes only by eliminating personal weaknesses through self-knowledge and experience – and even then we can never always be in full control. As I mused, I saw Arnold hit his approach into the right-hand bunker. Not a serious problem, really, because I had been there only minutes earlier and saved par. But quite suddenly Arnold's nightmare began. His recovery was much too fierce and the ball raced to the back of the green. He was now a shaken man and perhaps not quite in control because his chip shot stopped 5 yards from the hole. Now he needed this putt to tie with me. And he missed. The Great Man had taken six and I was a surprised and grateful Masters champion.

While such traumas invariably occur in the last moments of a championship and add to the theatrical impact of the occasion, I am convinced they are also as much part of the test of a champion as any question of stroke-making. Winning a championship is a complete trial of skill and character, particularly over the longer haul when the collection of titles increases year by year. At this level, perhaps the most important quality is an ability to cope with adversity in all its forms. Crazy as it seems, it even has to be enjoyed.

There is a genuine pain factor in success: a curious torment when under pressure that makes you yearn to escape and run for cover while knowing you must go through with it, otherwise you could never live with the thought that you had given up. I knew a young talented golfer once who could play so brilliantly that he would force himself into contention and then somehow score a double-bogey after which, with the pressure removed, he would bounce back magnificently with a couple of birdies to finish among the leaders and declare: 'If only I hadn't taken that double-bogey!' The truth was that subconsciously he *wanted* that double-bogey because it removed him from the pain of winning. I have heard jockeys talk about a similar characteristic in horses: how it might seem to the punter that a horse is doing its best and almost neck-and-neck with the leader, but the rider knows – he feels – the horse is dwelling and not giving everything down that final furlong. It lacks heart.

When one considers the pieces of the puzzle that go to make up a champion, I believe that this enjoyment of adversity is of major significance. Jack Nicklaus calls it his idea of fun. Ask him his ideal moment and he will say: 'Three holes to play, and a birdie and two pars to win.' The personal challenge in all of this is in some way the main attraction. It is the process of winning, absolute self-control at exactly the right moment in terms of judgement and skill, that is the true prize. What comes afterwards – the trophy, the prize money and the acclaim – are somehow less important than the actual process of winning and the memory of it afterwards. After all, ask any great champion what he remembers of a famous victory. It certainly will not be the speech he made afterwards or how he spent the prize money. Rather, he will recall an instant – one shot perhaps – which turned the proceedings his way.

For me, there have been several such well-documented moments, the first of which was the stroke I played with a fairway wood to a green I could not see which unquestionably earned me the British Open at Carnoustie in 1968. I had arrived at the Scottish links a week early in the hope of getting to know the course in the way Ben Hogan had done back in 1953 when he won the title. I told waiting journalists I still had not given myself enough time to learn all I needed to know. Hogan even walked the course from green to tee in the evenings just to get a different perspective on the landing areas. Carnoustie was an awesome test measuring 7,252 yards, the longest Open championship course at that time, and it required power and precision; yet curiously enough both Billy Casper and Bob Charles, not noted for their length, led the way until that final round.

In a way I was glad to be paired with Jack Nicklaus on the final afternoon because I suspected he would become the major threat and at least I could keep an eye on him. For the first two rounds I felt I had played rubbish. Then, on the practice ground, I discovered I was moving laterally in my attempts to hit the ball hard and had become very erratic. I just told myself to 'stay back' on the shot as I hit the ball and sure enough the old snap and precision came back into my stroke-making. However, I was still not happy with my putting even though I had phoned home to Johannesburg before the championship and asked Vivienne to bring over my favourite blade putter with her.

Despite such problems, I had moved within reach of the leaders who, I suspected, could become vulnerable. What surprised me was that Jack himself seemed unsettled and not quite in control. On the long sixth he hooked his tee shot out of bounds on to the rifle range and was so angry he kicked his golf bag hard enough to remove it from his caddie Jimmy Dickinson's grasp. But I was still worried about Jack as we played the long fourteenth, even though he was two strokes behind and I was tied with Casper and Charles for the lead. I remember repeating to myself: 'I must beat this guy. I know I can beat this guy.' For me this contest had resolved itself into a duel between myself and Jack, and we revelled in the moment.

His tee shot slipped away towards the trees on the right and I had hit my golf ball into the fairway, but my view of the green was blocked by the ridge with its two bunkers called 'The Spectacles' from which the hole gets its name. Jack fashioned a magnificent stroke from the trees and we waited to hear how the crowd responded because neither of us could see the green. It was a gathering cheer which grew in strength to a roar, then stopped. Jack was safely on. Now it was my turn. When I settled over the ball all I could see was the ridge and its bunkers looming ahead of me. I started the backswing, hit and then waited. The roar started again and I ran to the top of the hill. I said afterwards that the ball was travelling so perfectly on line 'I had to lean sideways to see the top of the flag.'

Vivienne was behind the green. So too was Henry Cotton, and he held his hands apart to show me I was only 2 feet from the hole. The eagle three was a formality and I had broken the deadlock. When it was over Jack was first to congratulate me on the last green.

I leave it to others to ponder on the nature and source of such a match-winning stroke; how and why the exact result emerges when nothing else will do; or how I could have played perhaps twenty more strokes from that position and not despatched the ball so close to the flag again. It is, I suppose, a response to the moment, to the excitement, the adrenalin – and perhaps also to being able to focus on what I considered to be my main task: that of beating Jack on the other side of the fairway, although it has not always been essential for me to have a specific opponent in my sights to produce winning form.

In 1972 it looked as though I had squandered a golden chance of winning the American PGA championship at Oakland Hills when I let a three-stroke lead slip away on the final day. By the time I reached the sixteenth I was tied for the lead but clearly under intense pressure. There were ten of us bunched tightly together and I kept telling myself I did not want to finish second again in a major championship. I hated the prospect. I had just missed a tiny putt on the fifteenth green. I tried to put the memory of the error out of my mind, but it did not quite work because I then hit a tee shot which drifted to the right behind a willow tree on the edge of a lake which protected the green. I was confronted by the fearsome task of getting the ball airborne quickly enough to clear the tree and imparting sufficient power to carry the ball to a flagstick I could not see.

The flag was on the right-hand side and close to the water, so there was little margin for error. I knew I had a shot of 152 yards and that from the fairway I could have taken a comfortable eight iron to get home. But that club was quite useless for this task. I knew I needed a nine iron. I looked at the grass around the lie and realized it was wet, which meant the ball would jump a little when it was struck and give me extra distance. Then I peered under the tree and saw a seat stick that had been left by a spectator. It was on perfect line to the flag and I made it my target. I took out the nine iron, aimed, and struck the ball as hard as I could. In such a moment there is a cold realization that there is nothing more to be done than to trust the swing and all those relentless hours of practice that disciplined it. There was time only to check the grip, the stance, then aim – and fire. I waited as the ball cleared the tree and disappeared from my view. Then I heard the cheers. When I emerged from behind the tree the ball was only 4 feet from the flagstick. I holed out for a birdie three and went on to win the title by two shots. To the onlooker it may have seemed an effortless demonstration of judgement and skill, but it required the pressure of that moment – that bleak awareness that nothing else but this precise shot would do – to trigger the act.

In the process of winning, I sense at times an unspoken acknowledgement – but more than just a hope – that this really is 'going to be my day'. This is particularly emphasized in a golf tournament because there is time to think, dwell and consider between shots and rounds. Moreover, there is a curious spiritual aspect that seems to attach itself to this game and, I suspect, is experienced by all winners. I remember Max Faulkner explaining the feeling he had before playing the final day of the 1951 British Open, which he won: 'It was quite eerie. I seemed to know – really know – before the final day that no matter how many bad strokes I played, no matter what the problem, I would come through to be champion. It was a feeling of enormous strength. I felt caught up by a spirit and power much greater than myself. I never felt it again.' Rarely does a professional talk about these private moments, yet I think it is important to pass them on to others. That is why I talked about my 'vision' during the 1965 US Open at Bellerive in St Louis, which some people later passed off as a condition somewhere between self-hypnosis and hysteria. I 'saw' my name on the giant scoreboard beside the last green before I won the title. I saw it there all week. Of course I kept the experience secret at the time. There was a list of previous winners on the scoreboard and, to other people, the space against the year 1965 was blank. What I saw in gold lettering was the name Gary Player. Only when I had beaten Kel Nagle in the play-off did I reveal the story.

Clearly there is more to winning at sport than simply the physical skills involved. My personal experiences throughout my career suggest a deeper side in which the power of mind over matter really does have some relevance. Was I looking into the future when I 'saw' my name on the board? Or was it some kind of self-induced state? I will admit that I was obsessed with winning the US Open and that the thought preoccupied much of my time. In any case that particular drama was of a personal nature and went unnoticed. It was an altogether different story when I won the British Open at Royal Lytham St Annes in 1974 by surviving two extraordinary crises over the closing holes while the world looked on. As I played the seventeenth it seemed that nothing could stop me because I was six strokes clear of my nearest rival and within sight of the clubhouse and my third British title. The grass behind the seventeenth green was long and thick and I remember saying to my caddie 'Rabbit' Dyer during practice: 'Anybody who hits over there is dead. That's one place we don't ever want to go.' Perhaps it was a moment's lapse of concentration or the thought of victory just round the corner, but the result was that I struck my approach exactly where I did not want to go and into the long grass behind the green. As we walked towards the green I wondered whether we would ever find the ball, even though there were officials and spectators all around.

The first thing I did was to ask an official to put the watch on me to observe the five-minute search rule. I was in full view of the television cameras and hundreds of fans. Imagine winning the British Open and then somebody claiming that I went seven seconds over my allotted five-minute search time! After all, it is a unique aspect of golf that anybody anywhere in the world who spots a rules infringement during the progress of play can report it and have official action taken. There was an incident in the 1982 Open at Troon when Tony Jacklin was spotted by a television viewer making an incorrect drop from a bush. The error was quite unintentional but he was penalized when the matter was reported. Paul Azinger was playing in the Doral

Ryder Open in Miami when a television viewer in Colorado thought he spotted an unwitting infringement as Paul played from a hazard. The video tape was re-run: the viewer was correct and Paul was disqualified. Thus the question of correct procedure is always important. I remember once leading a tournament in Memphis when my golf ball came to rest in ground under repair. A PGA official told me where to drop the ball but my playing partner Hubert Green disputed the decision. I was so angry I said: 'Hubert, where would you like me to drop it? If you want me to drop it in a divot I will do so.' The official was not amused and warned: 'Gary, if you don't drop where I tell you, I will penalize you.' End of story. We did as we were told and followed the proper procedure.

For that reason, that day at Lytham I put the watch on myself. It was a frantic search in which I even got down on my hands and knees looking for the ball. I asked everybody around me to join in the hunt but it still seemed like a hopeless task, even though so many people had been only a few feet from the spot where it landed. There was barely a minute of the search time left when a marshal found the ball. It still looked a formidable task for me even to finish the hole. I took a full swing and moved the ball only a few feet but at least the lie was better and I chipped and single putted for an astounding bogey five.

Even then the drama was not over, because I hit my approach clear through the last green and up against the wall of the clubhouse. For me, this should have been the time for the famous march to glory, acknowledging the thousands of fans in the grandstands as I moved to the last green. But here was Gary Player in customary peril and nobody was quite sure how this particular episode would end. The ball was only inches from the wall, so it could not be played right-handed. Officials decided the clubhouse was an integral part of the course and therefore I was not entitled to a free drop. The ball had to be played where it lay or I could take a drop under penalty. I decided to play left-handed with the back of my putter; the ball popped slightly in the air and finished 10 feet short of the hole. I took two putts to hole out and win the title by four shots from Peter Oosterhuis.

On reflection it is possible to take a more reasoned view that a six-stroke lead eased any serious pressure over those closing holes. But hindsight is a very precise science. As that drama unfolded, I did not know how it would end and that uncertainty made every move extremely crucial. I had finished bogey-bogey to become champion. Strange game, really – Jack Nicklaus finished that same stretch with a brace of bogeys in the 1963 Open and he lost the title by a stroke.

It has been a pattern of my victories to find myself repeatedly slugging it out toe-to-toe with other contenders for the title, but in fact I caught them all napping in 1978 with a surprise last round run when I covered the back nine at Augusta in thirty strokes for a 64 and – not for the first time in my career – had to wait to see if anybody could catch me. Three men came to the last green with a chance to force me into a play-off. But all of them – Tom Watson, Rod Funseth and Hubert Green (who missed from inside 3 feet) – failed. How appropriate it was that day that I should be partnered by Seve Ballesteros, who was born in 1957, the year I made my Masters debut, and that he should thereafter become such a dominant figure at Augusta – even if he did not win all the chances that came his way.

That Masters victory gave me the thought that perhaps I would win a major title in a fourth decade as we moved into the 1980s; and in truth I was runner-up in the 1984 American PGA Championship at Shoal Creek in Birmingham, Alabama, but despite a second round 63, I was always just too far out of reach to catch the irrepressible Lee Trevino. Still, we had both proved a point: that nobody can ever really be written off in this game. It is always full of surprises. It is the reason I am still eager to tee up week after week. Who knows, it could just be my day . . .

CHAPTER 3
The Big Three . . . and Other Heroes

There is a curious theory that the title of 'Big Three' accorded to Arnold Palmer, Jack Nicklaus and myself at the height of our careers was nothing more than a clever sales gimmick for a series of television golf matches between us. The record books suggest a different and more obvious reason for the accolade and may lead future historians to regard our domination of golf during the 1960s as probably the most influential period in its development as we brought the sport to a wider audience. It has already been regarded by some contemporary observers as being of equal significance to the impact of the Great Triumvirate – J. H. Taylor, Harry Vardon and James Braid – on the game at the beginning of the twentieth century. Together, it is fair to say we lifted professional golf into the big league in terms of commercial appeal and individual earning power. What Arnold had started in his charismatic solo way by giving the game an aggressive excitement to match other spectator sports, we broadened through the contests we fought against each other on and off the screen.

It is an historical fact that great rivalries in sport – whether in tennis, golf, athletics or motor racing – prompt each protagonist to ever greater achievements and in so doing lift the standard of their pursuit to new levels which others are obliged to follow. So it was with the Big Three. With no disrespect to our contemporaries, when we teed up in major contests we sensed we were playing against each other, even though we knew that the other players could slip in and grab the title. But it was that kind of domination that prompted fellow professionals, as they played, to look at the scoreboard to see what the Big Three were doing.

A cursory glance at the records shows that for seven successive years from 1960, one of the Big Three won the US Masters. Of the twenty-eight major championships played in that period, the Big Three won fifteen. Only four men in the history of the game have ever captured the Grand Slam of the world's four major titles and two of them – Jack and myself – were members of the Big Three.

Moreover, in 1962 we held all four major titles at once: Arnold was US Masters and British Open champion; Jack had captured the US Open; and I was American PGA champion.

Thus the title Big Three was much more than a television trademark, even though it did irritate other professionals and prompted Gay Brewer, after winning the US Masters in 1967, to declare: 'There's no Big Three. At least not as far as Gary Player is concerned.' Later that year, Gay and I clashed during the World Matchplay championship in a curious encounter that had an extraordinary conclusion because our match went to extra holes when Brewer, gazing into the fading gloom, realized the hole had been placed in a new position by the green-keeping staff in readiness for the next day's play. He insisted it be replaced in its former position, even though we had played the two previous extra holes without noticing the switch. The referee Michael Bonallack, now secretary of the Royal and Ancient Club of St Andrews, borrowed a pen-knife to start re-cutting the hole in its original position and when the ritual was completed we played on and I won the hole and the match.

I told the press afterwards: 'I admit I was playing with a little more determination today. Gay has said some nasty things about me in the past. But I'll say one thing. He is a very good player.' He is also now a very good friend on the Seniors Tour. Those wilful days are far behind both of us and long forgotten. Even so, his reaction was typical of many top professionals of the period to the public image Arnold, Jack and myself had forged. Perhaps too, there was a tinge of envy of the three of us – that even though we played so hard against each other we remained truly firm and close friends. I think each of us brought special qualities to the alliance that went beyond the neat adversarial roles that the public beheld – two big-hitting American heroes and one little foreigner who managed not only to keep up with them but could beat them man-to-man.

I first saw Arnold on the practice ground of the Tam O'Shanter tournament in 1957. It was my first visit to the United States and I just stood and watched him in awe as he hit practice shots, because in truth I had never seen the ball hit with such power. Nor had I ever seen such a strong pair of hands in my life. His grip on the club was the best: those huge wrists and forearms gave him such immense power. I used to joke that when he hit the ball I saw sparks coming off the grass. As I progressed on the US Tour so we became friends and Arnold was totally enthusiastic when his agent Mark McCormack asked whether it would be a good idea if he were to manage me too. Later we were joined by Jack Nicklaus when he turned professional.

What is remarkable is that irrespective of money and success, we liked being together. There was an intensely close rapport among us which eliminated any possibility of bitterness or envy at the other man's achievements. What we had was an intense rivalry balanced by a enormous respect for one another as men and as players. It was as though there was a secret unspoken rule. We were the best of friends, yet we always accepted that we wanted to beat the hell out of each other on the golf course and that we would play as hard and as tough as we could to achieve that aim. But whatever the outcome, it was all left there on the last green.

It spilled over just once between Arnold and myself, not too many years ago. We had an argument at his club called Bay Hill in Orlando. And the experience was so upsetting that both of us ended up in tears. Quite unbelievable really, the macho men of golf crying over something that had been said. It was not as if either of us had a chance to win the tournament. However, what struck home to each of us was that we had overstepped the mark that had been there throughout our careers. We realized we had broken the code that had existed between us for all that time. We made it up, of course, and vowed never to make the mistake again. It was a stupid argument anyway. I had finished badly in his tournament, dropping four shots in the last two holes, and had made some sarcastic remark about the course he had re-designed. He hit back. I think we went into his office to finish the row. It was a rather petty episode and that also somehow made it all the more distressing.

We had travelled all over the world together – South Africa, Australia, Japan, Europe. Those years were a great period in my life. I learned much from Arnold, not only about golf but more about the responsibilities that are part of being a public hero. He is a man who always acknowledged his duty to his fans. I have watched him come off the course after scoring an 80 and an hour later he was still standing there signing autographs for his devoted followers. That is a measure of his enormous patience and also a reflection of his great importance to American sports fans – who to this day, I suspect, would still prefer to watch Arnie shoot 80 than somebody else score in the low 60s. In fact, nobody really cares about the score. They want to see this man for what he is – their hero. I have occasionally seen my good friend Seve Ballesteros push past his fans after a bad round. I have watched Tom Weiskopf become irritated by autograph hunters. I admit that at first the paper-and-pencil brigade irritated me when I just wanted to work hard on the practice ground. But when I saw Arnold take all the time in the world for his public, I knew he was right.

He loves golf. He loves playing it much more than Jack and I will ever do. He loves to tinker with clubs. That aspect has never appealed to me. I do not have a huge collection of clubs. I have two sets: one in regular use and a replacement set in case the others get lost. All this fiddling with clubs, taping, altering lies, grips and angles, frankly bores me.

On reflection, I think that one of the reasons we have remained such strong friends is that we never talked about one another's comparative wealth; we know that Arnold is the richest of us all but there has never been any question of jealousy because of it. Whenever the three of us played an exhibition match I never asked what fee Arnold and Jack were getting. I asked for my fee and that was all that concerned me. I accept Arnold's importance and our relative pulling power. Arnold has huge sales appeal, not simply because of his success and the aggressive way he played, but more for the integrity he exudes. The Palmer name has been used to sell a variety of products from golf clubs to sunglasses. At one time, it helped to launch a franchise of dry-cleaning stores on the basis that everybody knew Arnie and knew they would receive good service. For that reason, too, he is one of the most successful car dealers in the United States. Yet he has always observed a very conservative way of life. He has never been a man of extravagance. Even though he loves flying, his personal jet is not simply a luxury but is used for charter work when he is not using it. He has brought his children up with impeccable manners and they have not been spoiled because their father was one of the richest and most famous sportsmen in the world. Arnie is a strict disciplinarian but much of the credit too for his happy family must to to his wife, Winnie, who gave him the support and the peace of mind to pursue his career to the top.

In fact, all three of us are well aware of the vital roles our wives have played in our careers. Without their constant and unquestioning help, I wonder what would have happened to us. I always believe that Winnie Palmer, Barbara Nicklaus and Vivienne Player are the real Big Three because they have endured so much sacrifice in our pursuit of success.

Jack is a fervent family man. During a tournament, he once flew back from Mexico City to Florida in his own jet on successive nights to watch his children playing in an important college basketball match. The round trip brought him back to Mexico City in the wee small hours, and he did not play well but he had honoured his promise to his kids. Jack never worries about time-keeping and this used to irritate Arnold, who is an extremely punctual man. I sometimes suspected that Jack deliberately arrived late for some of our matches just to irritate the hell out of Arnold. It was an amazing foible, really, because tournament golf, with its precise starting times and penalties, insists on punctuality, and yet, if Jack said he would meet for a game at 11 o'clock in the morning, his partners could be in for a wait.

The only other man I ever knew with a similar cavalier attitude to time-keeping was Bobby Locke, my fellow countryman. He was a great golfer and gentleman who loved his beer, singing songs and playing poker dice. We once fixed up to play a practice round at Wentworth when I was a young newcomer and I arrived eagerly two hours early to practice. Our tee-time arrived and went and there was no sign of Bobby. An hour later he was still absent, and after a further fifteen-minute wait I decided to tee off. Suddenly I heard a familiar voice: 'What's this, Master? Are you teeing off without me?' Bobby had arrived. I said it was well past our agreed starting time and he smiled: 'Don't worry about it, Master. We've got all day!' He was in any case a man who measured his pace of life in slow and deliberate fashion. He never hurried; he even shaved slowly. He walked slowly and hit fewer practice shots than any other player of his class. He was perhaps the most tranquil champion of them all.

It might seem quite astonishing in a way that Arnold and Jack ever became such firm friends because in the early days Nicklaus was seen by sports fans as the unwelcome and unpopular threat to their beloved Arnie. He was the victim of all kinds of abuse and some fans even tried to intimidate him. At tournaments they would stand in the rough and hold up placards which said 'Hit it here, Ohio Fats!' In those days I remember one practice round we played together at Augusta. We were walking along the third hole and the fans simply cheered for Arnold. Jack hit his approach close and the people hardly applauded. For Arnold they went wild when he just made the green with his approach. And so it went on until the last hole when Jack bogeyed and they cheered. Jack turned to me and said quietly: 'The more they do that, the more I will beat him.'

Not that Arnold had any control over the antics of his fans, nor did Jack hold him responsible. But I think what Jack perceived in the rapport that Arnold had with the crowds was that it had nothing to do with hitting the ball close to the pin. It was the way he gave himself to the public they loved. He is a great giver. Jack, on the other hand, could be immensely single-minded, to the point of immovable stubbornness, and he admits freely that this trait probably has something to do with his Germanic ancestry. When I played Jack I knew he revelled in being a long-hitter and that he could be a bit hard-headed and believed that what he was doing was absolutely right.

The incident with Colonel Tony Duncan in the 1966 World Matchplay championship was a prime example of Jack in his most stubborn mood. He disputed a ruling from the referee and caused the ex-army officer to quit on the spot. It happened at the ninth hole and I was his opponent, though I decided to stay well clear of this altercation. Jack had hooked into a ditch, then noticed that an advertising sign 100 yards ahead of him was on his line of play to the green. He asked for a free drop but Colonel Duncan refused. Jack asked for a rule-book and insisted he was right. The referee simply walked away. I was not getting involved in this one. My shot was already on the green. Jack tried to hit the ball free but moved it only a few yards and conceded the hole. On the next tee, Colonel Duncan said: 'Would you like to have another referee?' Jack replied: 'I would like to have one who knows the rules.' Duncan could take no more. Gerald Micklem, an acknowledged rules expert, was asked to referee the rest of the match. To this day Jack is convinced he was absolutely right in his interpretation of the rules because there are few people in the world with a greater knowledge of them. But I think it still niggles him that he caused a referee to quit. That simply should not happen in sport. The referee's word must be final.

At the end of the day he was beaten and I became champion again. But what I remember most about that day was the manful way Jack took his defeat and the tribute he paid to me when he said: 'I don't think anybody living could have played better than Gary did today.' He also showed his capacity to put things like defeat into perspective. He had played very erratically and told the crowds: 'Thank you all for your support. I know how difficult it was for you all to thread your way through the woods on either side of the fairway. I know because I was in there often enough myself today.'

Jack is a man of great courage and I suspect that one of the greatest rounds of his life came in 1986 on the final day of the US Masters when he slipped past everybody with some brilliant play to win the title. He was then 46 years old but few people knew that there was more at stake than simply the pride of a middle-aged man. His business empire had run into problems because a couple of golf course projects had soured. He was a deeply worried man, and in fact I learned later that a magazine had actually sent a team of writers to Augusta to write a story about the fall of the Nicklaus empire. But all that changed with the magnificent last-round 64 which earned him his sixth Masters title and made him once again the nation's hero. It was enough to restore the wider credibility he needed and to attract the necessary commercial support that saw him through the crisis and on to better times.

As a player, he was not the best striker I have ever seen. But he was the best thinker. Nobody ever prepared better for an event than Jack and he possessed an incredible ability to make the right decision when he played. He thought his way round the course. I remember one practice round when it seemed he could not keep a drive on the fairway and I said: 'Having problems?' Jack said: 'Not really. I am just seeing what sort of liberties I can take with the rough.' That was a measure of his preparedness. He wanted to know the exact margin of error he could allow himself from the tee and the sort of lie he might find. But the fact is nobody else but Jack Nicklaus could give that sort of answer – and mean it.

Of course, it has to be said that even legends occasionally enjoy a bit of horseplay and I remember on one occasion it got slightly out of hand when the three of us were sharing a plush hotel suite in Canada. Arnold was on the phone to his wife Winnie when for some reason I decided to shake a bottle of beer and squirt it all over him. Jack started to laugh so I turned round and let him have it too. Now they were both after me. Jack picked up a jug of iced tea and hurled the contents towards me. I ducked and the liquid drenched the curtains. Rather sheepishly, we had to call the hotel manager and tell him the Big Three owed him for a new set of curtains. We told him there had been a mishap.

Silly, of course, but it indicated the bond of friendship that existed and still does exist between us. I can honestly say that I love the two of them. I have competed against them, tried to beat the hell out of them and did not feel sorry for them when I did because I knew they would not when I was losing. That was the understanding we had. Win or lose, it was nothing personal. But then that applies to most of the golfers I have played. There are not many whom I positively dislike or who have upset me enough to warrant a nasty memory. Some have personalities which are not always easy to understand or handle but that is no cause for disdain.

I found Peter Thomson to be a highly intelligent man and one of the brightest golfers I have ever met. He was well travelled and well read but he was aloof and could be very sarcastic at times. It always seemed to me that he wanted to reveal his superiority and knowledge to people. One story illustrates the point. The 1963 Canada Cup in France was delayed for a day because of fog, after which I had to make a desperate dash all the way to Melbourne to compete in the Australian Open. The route took me more than twenty-nine hours' flying time via New York, Los Angeles, Hawaii and Sydney until I reached Melbourne at 10 o'clock in the morning. There was just time for me to shower then I had to use a new set of clubs and revert to the smaller-size golf ball. I won the championship in what was the most amazing triumph of my career but all Peter said afterwards was: 'What's so amazing about that? You were sitting down and resting all the time on the aeroplane, weren't you?'

He was a very over-rated golfer but I would say he was the best I have ever seen with the small golf ball on a firm links course. That was his stage. Elsewhere he did not impress me. He had a dismissive attitude in those days towards American golf. He seemed to regard it as nothing more than power play, lacking artistry, and Arnold Palmer as its personification. Not surprisingly, they did not get on. In fact, when Arnold faced Peter in the final of the 1968 World Matchplay championship he said: 'We Americans always like to win but I guess you can say we take particular pleasure in beating Peter.' True to his word, Arnold triumphed in a glorious and close-fought final from which I suspect both men emerged with new respect for each other.

In a personal way I have always considered Lee Trevino to be part of our group because of his achievements and status; perhaps if he had arrived on the scene a little earlier we would have been known as the Big Four. I admire him because, quite apart from his skills, he is a worker and he is irrepressible. I once called his hotel room and clearly it was the morning after a convivial evening.

I said: 'Is that Lee Trevino?'

A bleary voiced answered: 'Wait a minute. Let me look in the mirror.'

There was a paused.

'Yep. It's me all right.'

Lee came from a poor background like myself, earned himself a fortune, then lost his money in a property deal that went wrong – but bounced back to make another fortune. He has been married three times. He has no regrets: Lee never looks back. He probably loves golf even more than Arnold does, and once remonstrated with me for all my other commitments – golf course design and so on – and said: 'Man, I don't want any of this golf course design business. When I wake up in the morning all I want to do is slap that rubber ball.' On another occasion he told me: 'You don't know what pressure is like until you have a dollar in your pocket and you are playing for five hundred. I had to hustle. I know what it takes to win and what it costs to lose.' And he once paid me the greatest compliment when he said: 'This guy is grinding even when he is making a ten.'

There are two other judgements I will treasure for the rest of my life. Arnold once said that I was the greatest competitor he had ever seen. Jack told me that the greatest performance he had ever witnessed on a golf course was my round in front of all the civil rights activists when my life was under threat during the 1969 American PGA championship in Dayton, Ohio.

Looking back, what can be said is that The Big Three came along at exactly the right time in the history of golf and that we set standards and trends – particularly with our attendance at the British Open, for example – which all players for generations to come must follow if they wish to stand comparison. It was not about money. I won more prize money in a couple of years on the American Seniors Tour than I collected in my entire playing career on the regular circuit. Pretty soon Jack Nicklaus will slip down the list of all-time money winners. The irony is that this man who has won twenty major titles will soon be left far behind Tom Kite, heading towards his sixth million by 1991 but who at that time did not even have one major title to his credit. Gene Sarazen got it right when he said the only relevant question to be asked of a man's career was: 'How many majors did you win?' It placed everybody in their correct order of importance, particularly the multiple winners who had proved their rare ability to aim at the big occasions. In those terms the Big Three made its mark with a total of thirty-six titles.

Whatever else, it means that the lists of winners of the four major championships reveal a period when the names of Palmer, Player and Nicklaus appear with intriguing regularity. This might prompt some enthusiast in the future to want to know more about how and why three men from different backgrounds came to dominate the game and form an unbreakable bond of friendship. We have all moved on. Jack heads up his own Golden Bear International. Arnold and I also head our own respective business organizations but remain linked loosely through our continuing involvement with Mark McCormack, who initially brought us all together. The bond remains strong. We still enjoy each others' company. We are still ready to do any favour required. What we share is the memory of the contribution we made to the game of golf. It is an epitaph we are happy to settle for – all three of us. Future historians, please note.

CHAPTER 4
The Watson Affair and Other Skirmishes

In November 1983 I suddenly found myself embroiled in the nastiest incident of my career when it became public knowledge that Tom Watson had accused me of infringing the rules of golf.

I was staggered that such an accusation could be made. My championship career spanned a quarter of a century. I had joined Gene Sarazen and Ben Hogan as only the third man in history to win the Grand Slam of four major world titles. I had won more than 150 tournaments worldwide including a total of nine majors. Yet now it was being suggested that I had broken the rules. Moreover, I was being accused in the presence of two of the great names of the sport – Jack Nicklaus and Arnold Palmer – both of whom I counted as friends and had respected as players and men of honour all the years I had known them.

It was a truly sorry affair in which the accusation was not made until I had left the golf course and the game was over. It took me totally by surprise, not least because the correct procedure according to the rules would have been to raise the matter at the time. I was astonished that Tom, who has collaborated with the United States Golf Association on a book about the rules of golf, did not adopt the correct procedure.

My judgement on Tom was that he had an outstanding temperament and a wonderful short game. But I think what he did to me that day will haunt him for the rest of his life. Breaking the rules is, after all, the most heinous charge to be laid against any golfer. When it is aimed at a champion, the repercussions can be monumental.

It is essential to the proper conduct of the game that players observe a strict code of personal honesty. Not only is it important because the cross-country nature of the game makes it impossible to scrutinize every action, but the absence of a referee imposes an even greater burden of responsibility on a player. Thus the most important quality of all on a golf course must be personal integrity and a strict observance of the rules. In fact, the personal challenge of the game itself demands a kind of morality of such high and constant standard that those who falter soon become disenchanted and move to some other sport where the responsibility for good order is placed upon the referee. This sets golf apart, even when thousands of spectators – perhaps millions via television – are on hand to watch a player's every action at the closest range. It means that even though the eyes of the world are observing, the player himself has sole responsibility for his own conduct on the field of play.

Poor Roberto de Vicenzo, the delightful Argentinian professional, discovered that important truth to his cost when millions saw him score a birdie three on the seventeenth hole at Augusta in the 1968 Masters, but in his haste at the end of play, he signed for a par-four written on his card by his playing partner Tommy Aaron. Under the rules that higher score had to stand, so Roberto missed a chance of the play-off by a stroke he never made and Bob Goalby became champion even though he had not scored better. But then rules are rules.

Without doubt, this uncompromising code is one of the strengths of the game. We are all bound by these fundamental rules, even if at times the tournament player receives special dispensations to cope with the problems incurred by certain factors – sanctions to take free drops away from TV towers, cables and advertising signs, for example. And what makes it work for all of us is the knowledge that we all conduct ourselves according to these rules and we trust each other implicitly to do so. If we sense an error or even a doubt in our conduct then we report it. I have invoked the rules against myself on several occasions during my career when I discovered I was wrong. Such decisions were always immediate: I did not hesitate. I remember during the Greater Greensboro Open I had walked 10 yards away from the scorer's tent and could not remember whether I had signed my card. I was leading the tournament at the time with one round to play having just scored 67. I went back and checked. I had not signed the card. I reported the matter to Jack Tuthill, the PGA official, who told me that, regretfully, I was disqualified. There was an amusing footnote to this episode: when I told fellow South African Pete Matkovitch, who was working as my caddie, what had happened he joked: 'Don't tell me. Tell my lawyer. That was the best chance I had in a long time of making money!'

Then, too I was playing in a team match with Bob Charles on the Seniors Tour and we had reached only the second hole when I was convinced we had made a mistake in the alternate-shot form we were supposed to be playing. I called an official. Sure enough, we had got it wrong and were disqualified. Once, in the Colonial event in Texas, I discovered I had too many clubs in my bag and reported myself, and on another occasion in Tampa I called a penalty on myself when my ball moved as I addressed it even though nobody else noticed.

It is simply the code by which we live. I remember Tom Weiskopf taking what he thought was a legitimate free drop from a cart path in the tournament at Hilton Head and when a doubt was raised – by a television viewer who phoned in – he took officials out to the spot to show them what he had done only to find he had adopted the wrong procedure and had to be disqualified. All of them genuine errors, but evidence, too, of how immediately players respond to the problems and how eager they are to ensure that the spirit of the game is upheld. At least, that is how I considered it until Watson made his accusation that day in Arizona.

I have to say on a personal level that I have never warmed to Tom as a person. I found him too dour. In fact, when we were both under contract to the Ram Corporation I requested that we conduct our golf clinics individually because I found no enjoyment working with him. There was a sharp personal edge to be seen and at times a disregard for the courtesies that normally exist between professionals. For example, it made little difference in playing terms to me when he hired Alfie Fyles, who had been my caddie for many years in Britain: all I would say is that I would never dream of approaching, say, Arnold's or Jack's caddie without first conferring with the player to find out whether it was in order to do so. No such contact was made with me over the Fyles transfer, although Alfie and I remain good friends.

Moreover, I had to confront Tom about another issue when it came to my attention that rumours were circulating about an alleged incident that was supposed to have occurred between us during a Canadian tournament. I was staggered to learn from my fellow South African Dale Hayes that there was talk that Tom had refused to sign my score-card because, it was claimed, I had tapped down a spike mark on the green, which is strictly against the rules. PGA officials, so the story went, had to sign my card instead. I immediately phoned from South Africa and contacted Clyde Mangum, the PGA official in charge of the event. He was astonished at the allegations and declared: 'I have no knowledge of this. Gary, you signed your card. So did Tom.' I could not let the matter drop, and when I returned to the United States, I saw Tom on the practice ground at Sawgrass in

Florida, and tackled him. I said: 'There seems to be a bit of a rumour about you not signing my card and that PGA officials had to sign it. You accused me of knocking down a spike mark.' Tom was vehement that no such incident had occurred. I thought that was the end of the matter. There was just one other hurtful moment later when I learned that the Watson contingent had made some disparaging remark about Arnold Palmer and myself to the effect that as box-office stars we were has-beens. One of his management team made such a remark to my manager during the Skins Game in which we were playing. Nothing was said, but the attitude was noted.

This, then, was the background to the extraordinary Episode of the Leaf in which Watson accused me of breaking the rules but then found himself being criticized for his insensitive behaviour. All four of us – Tom, Jack, Arnold and myself – were featured in a Skins Game to mark the opening of the Desert Highlands course which Jack had designed just outside Phoenix. The event was spread over two days and was being filmed for television, quite apart from being watched at the resort by a substantial gallery of golf fans who followed us closely all the way.

The Skins Game system offers a sum of money to be won on each hole by the player with the lowest score. If two players have the same low score then the cash rolls over to the next hole, so that at times there can be some hefty sums involved, particularly in a tight match when many holes have been halved. So it was in this match, and by the time we reached the 224-yard sixteenth there were $120,000 at stake. Arnold hit his tee shot left of the green into rocks and knew he was out of the hole. Jack was on the green but some 60 feet short of the hole. Tom was just off the green and a little closer. I was on the right-hand edge about 40 feet away. Jack made a great attempt at his birdie putt and the ball lipped out to finish 18 inches away. Tom played a wonderful pitch shot to within a few inches. Thus both, virtually, had made their par-threes. Now it was my turn. Tom was standing about 8 yards away from me. The television cameras were on me and the crowds were within a few feet.

Watson subsequently made a statement to the UPI news agency in which he said:

> I observed Player attempting to reposition a growing live weed leaf from behind his ball to a different position. As I saw it, this was a breach of Rule 17.1 [now rule 13.1]. I consider abiding by the rules absolutely fundamental in playing the game of golf. As soon as I could

do so, I privately asked Joe Dey, the rules official, while walking up to the eighteenth fairway, if my understanding of the rules was correct.

I then asked him if he would be present at a very confidential meeting with Player after the match was concluded. He agreed. A meeting was held at the close of the match at which time I made my position known about the rules infraction and I considered the matter closed.

Unfortunately for all parties involved, what was to be a private meeting inadvertently has become a public matter. Golf has forty-one basic rules and hundreds of interpretations but essentially the rules can be reduced to three principles. One, play the ball as it lies. Two, play the course as you find it. Three, when it is not possible to do either, do what's fair.

One of the elements that makes golf truly distinctive is that it is a game played by the rules. I feel now, as I felt on Sunday that any breach of the rule, intended or unintended, must be resolved. If we overlook the rules then the game as we know it would become something much less than it is.

Well, Tom has had his word: and now it is time for mine.

Firstly, it was quite astonishing behaviour from a player of his calibre, because it should have occurred to him that the damaging aspect of the accusation was that it would always remain a question of personal word that could never be resolved to everybody's satisfaction and would therefore stand between us for the rest of our careers.

What he thought he saw was not actually correct. There certainly was grass behind the ball. I bent down, looked at it and moved it gently to see if it was attached. It was. That kind of thing happens quite often when a player checks to see if a piece of grass is dead or attached; it has to be tested in this way. This grass stayed where it was. The cameras were on us. I played the chip shot and nearly holed it. Not that it mattered, because Jack and Tom had halved the hole, which meant there were $170,000 to play for on the next hole. From the seventeenth fairway, I hit a wedge to 6 feet and sank the putt to scoop the pool and collect the biggest cheque of my career. But my joy was short-lived when I discovered that even though the match was over and nothing had been said during play, an allegation had been made and raised with our referee Joe Dey, the former US Tour Commissioner and USGA Executive Director, who was one of the world's acknowledged authorities on the rules of golf.

Jack and I went over to where Mr Dey and Watson were talking and it transpired that Watson claimed I had pressed down a growing leaf behind the ball. That was bad enough; but he then astounded me by bringing up the matter of his rumoured refusal to sign my score-card in the Canadian event over the spike mark business – an incident which he had assured me face-to-face had never happened! I insisted that the film of what happened on the sixteenth green should be re-run so that it would show exactly how wrong Tom had been. In fact a spokesman for the television production company said they had no idea there was any dispute but pointed out that if they had known anything about what was going on they would have put it on air immediately. But even then Watson could not let the matter rest and was quoted has saying: 'Whether Player was ignorant of the rule or was trying to improve his line of play is something within his heart. We'll never know.'

What surprised me was Tom's ignorance of the rules. It is quite clear that if he felt there had been an infringement, it should have been settled before we teed off on the next hole, or else he should have notified me under Rule 2(5) that he was lodging a claim to be settled later. Otherwise the matter was null and void and there could be no further discussion. The next day I read Watson quoted as saying: 'I didn't get much sleep last night thinking about it. I know this is a keg of dynamite. I know how reputations can be damaged. Some people will think it is sour grapes. One of the elements that makes golf truly distinctive is that it is a game played by the rules. My greatest regret is that this became public.' The glaring contradiction of that statement was that Tom, by not raising the issue at the appropriate moment, did not play to the rules.

The curious irony in all of this was that six years earlier it had been discovered that Tom had won major championships – the 1977 US Masters and British Open, beating Jack Nicklaus narrowly both times – with clubs that did not conform to the specification rules. The entire revelation was well documented in *The World of Professional Golf: Mark McCormack's Golf Annual 1978*. In reviewing the 1977 American PGA championship at Pebble Beach, McCormack referred to a topic that had been the major talking point at the Californian golf resort, and went on:

That concerned the legality of iron clubs, a controversy that surfaced at the Hartford Open the week before. During a practice round at

Hartford, Jerry Heard examined the clubs of George Burns, as pros are wont to do.

'Nice clubs you have there George,' said Heard. 'Too bad they're illegal.'

Heard had no way of knowing whether or not Burns' clubs were illegal, nor did it seem as if he were just needling Burns. But just in case, Burns asked Deputy Commissioner Clyde Mangum to inspect them. Mangum did and indeed Burns' clubs were illegal. The rules of golf state that the grooves on the face of irons 'shall not exceed 35/1000ths of an inch in width and shall not be any closer than three times that width'. Burns' grooves were too close.

So as the players arrived for the PGA their clubs underwent inspection – and were rejected in wholesale lots. Tom Watson lost all of his, Raymond Floyd had to get new ones and Gary Player had to change half of the irons in his bag. Watson, who plays Ram clubs, had a set of MacGregors he previously used shipped in and they too were declared illegal. The Ram Company admitted 'human error' in making custom clubs but not all of those rejected were manufactured by Ram.

Watson had won the Masters and the British Open using clubs found with illegal grooves. Some writers, perhaps facetiously, noted that all the money Watson had won with the fourteen-month-old clubs was tainted; indeed, that all he had won as a pro, including the 1975 British Open, should be erased because the only other clubs he had used were the MacGregors that were found to be faulty.

It took some of the glitter off the expected showdown between Watson and Jack Nicklaus. Watson and Nicklaus had gone head to head in the Masters and the British Open earlier in the year and Watson had emerged on top – both times.

True enough, there were some suggestions that no matter how innocently the error in the clubs had occurred, Tom ought to reconsider his position after discovering that he had been using the non-conforming clubs for fourteen months – one newspaper even suggested he hand back both titles, although I am not sure the runner-up Jack Nicklaus would have wanted them in such circumstances. But I often wonder how Jack felt about losing those two championships. I would hate to have won two of the world's major championships – the British Open and the Masters – knowing I had used illegally grooved clubs. I am pleased that is something I do not have to face up to in my golfing career.

What I find so distressing about the Arizona incident was that Tom did not voice his concern with me on the green. That would have

cleared the air. It happens all the time in golf. Players have queries
and they are settled. The reason he gave for not mentioning it at the
time was that he did not want to spoil the match. But he actually
spoiled a lot more by raising it wrongly afterwards. In fact he earned
himself more opprobrium for the manner of his allegation against me.
There was a lot of publicity and he knows that people did not like
what he did that day. Some of my fellow professionals reminded me
of an episode in the Tournament of Champions when he was overheard on television telling his playing partner Lee Trevino why he
was hooking the ball. Viewers heard that Tom thought Lee had the
ball too far forward in his stance and would do better to bring it back
a little. It was a well-intentioned act, no doubt, but Lee had not
sought help and Tom found that he was in breach of Rule 8 for giving
advice. He was penalized two strokes, yet still went on to win the
tournament – though it surprised many that he had infringed such a
basic rule.

Tom has some admirable qualities. I applauded him for the way he
resigned from his golf club in Kansas City when he discovered that a
Jew was being barred from potential membership. Tom's firm and
unequivocal stand against this act of anti-Semitism was successful and
the club changed its mind. I find it hard, therefore, for such a man to
be so quick to judge me. Was it sour grapes that day? I honestly do
not know. I know there have been players in the past who have lost to
me and then complained afterwards about the way I played. Some
even suggested that I used gamesmanship to win. But I can say
honestly that I have never used gamesmanship. Nor do I have much
respect for a professional who claims he has been a victim of it. A man
who complains about gamesmanship is a sissy. One of the reasons I
admire Jack Nicklaus so much is that he never looks for an excuse
when he loses. It is as though he echoes the sentiment of the great
Harry Vardon who, whenever he was beaten, would just simply say:
'That, sir, was the best I could do today!'

When I first came to Britain as a young professional in 1955 I
played at Sunningdale against Arthur Lees, a charming old individual
full of guile and skill. He was known as a very sharp man who had all
sorts of little tricks. We were playing the long tenth on the Old
Course and I could see that Arthur needed no more than a three iron
to reach the green. But he took out his three wood and I heard him
say quietly to his caddie: 'I'll joost coot it oop!' The idea was to fool
me into thinking I too needed a wood to reach the green and would
be too strong. He hit the most gorgeous shot. I heard him grunt as he

made contact. It was what we call a dead-wrist hit which requires brilliant feel, and sure enough the ball finished on the green. I admired what he had done, but I didn't fall for the trick. That would have made me an absolute fool. I am a professional, not a beginner.

I have found, regrettably, that there are some players who will take an instant dislike to people who have beaten them. Moreover, they find some excuse for their defeat other than the obvious fact that they were outplayed. When clashes of temperament occur, I regard them as the tensions of the moment. Nothing more sinister than that. They are inevitable when top sportsmen are giving everything for their chance to win. In these terms, I have found myself involved in several skirmishes over the years.

In the semi-final of the 1973 World Matchplay championship at Wentworth Johnny Miller accused me of gamesmanship. He claimed that I had deliberately taken four minutes to rake a bunker just to keep him waiting as he faced an important putt. It happened on the thirteenth hole. I was in a bunker on the right-hand side and my caddie had moved across to the left. I hit the ball close and even though Johnny was waiting to putt I raked the sand. It was ignorance on my part. I should have asked the caddie to come over and perform the task so that we could get on with the game. But it was a spur-of-the-moment decision on my part; Johnny thought it was deliberate and I did not blame him for thinking so. He told the press after he lost the match: 'If he wants to fix traps then he should not do it at my expense.' Some years later, I said to him: 'You know, I never tried that to keep you waiting deliberately.' And he said: 'Well, it sure looked like it.' He had a point.

It was certainly tension of the moment that prompted me to act wrongly against Tony Jacklin in the 1968 semi-final at Wentworth. I knew the crowd were pulling for Tony and it was understandable enough because he was the new hero and we had engaged in a marathon match that had gone the full thirty-six holes without a result and had to be postponed overnight because of bad light. The next morning I stood over a putt on the first extra hole and I could hear this person saying 'Miss it! Miss it!' I holed it and before Tony could hit his ball to save the match I went over to the guy and began to remonstrate with him. I tore into him, I was so uptight. Tony waited, stepped back and then missed his putt. There were a couple of boos.

What I did was completely wrong. I should have walked away. When I think of all the harassment I have had from crowds over the years, what happened at Wentworth was nothing. Instead, I over-reacted and let this chap have it. Tony and I never spoke about what happened. In mitigation I can only reflect that at times I react to the most curious incidents which seem to spur me into action. It was, after all, a chance remark I overheard between two spectators as I walked down the sixth fairway that really started my comeback against Tony Lema in 1964. This chap said to his pal: 'Come on, let's cut across to the eleventh hole. This match is over.' That is when I uttered my battle cry: 'Don't write me off.' The rest is history. My flare-up with the fan in 1968 may have had an effect on Tony Jacklin missing his putt. I don't know. All I do know is that I should have been more calm about it. I let myself down and should have had more discipline.

The confrontation with Graham Marsh in the 1973 final was another case of sheer tension. I like Graham and have much respect for him but I was taken aback that day as we walked from the seventeenth tee in the afternoon when he remarked that I had teed up in front of the markers on the tee. It seemed an odd time to remind me. If he had noticed an infringement on the tee, he could have said so at the time and even recalled the ball if he was so minded and made me play it again. It is, after all, a fairly innocent and common occurence in tournament golf and what normally happens is that a player is warned by his partner or opponent before he actually makes the stroke. It is strange how under such pressure, the mind focuses on some tiny point. I can remember even now placing my tee-peg in the same spot from which he had played on the tee. So if I was wrong, so was he. And I told him so. I am not sure which of us was more upset but I birdied the last hole to go to extra holes and beat him at the fortieth in what was then the longest and the closest match in the history of the championship. The other thought that struck me afterwards was that if we had both teed up beyond the marker, what possible difference would an inch or whatever have made on a long par-five hole measuring more than 500 yards?

For me, this was man to man stuff. What mattered to me above all else was the spirit of the game. It is probably a thought that Tom Watson can reflect upon in relation to that extraordinary, sad day in Arizona after which nothing between us could ever be the same again.

CHAPTER 5
'I Can Do All Things . . .'

There were a few sniggers from hard-bitten journalists when I explained during the press conference following my 1978 Masters win at Augusta that I had been uttering a silent prayer as I played the last round.

I revealed that throughout the drama of that afternoon I had repeated the quotation: 'I can do all things through Christ which strengtheneth me.' For the writers, it seemed to be the same old Gary Player deal with the Almighty. And yet the quotation held more than a grain of truth. At the start of that day I was just a name in the crowd; just one of the chorus line. I was the near-veteran who trailed seven strokes behind the leader and understandably nobody took any notice. That is, until they could see from the scoreboard that I was putting together what turned out to be a record-equalling 64 which may well have unnerved the leaders and led them into error because I was to win the title by a stroke and become the oldest man at the time ever to become Masters champion.

That day, as it was happening, I felt inspired and lifted and sensed that this was to be more than just a good round. I was assailed by that old feeling – almost an inexplicable insight – that no matter what everybody else did, the big prize was within my grasp. At this competitive level, golf is supposed to be a young man's game. I knew I was more than ten years older than the best of them: they were of another generation and yet I also knew I could 'do all things'. Afterwards, I could not keep quiet about it.

People either smile about the way I declare my faith in God when asked or feel rather awkward, perhaps impatient, about it and insist that the pursuit of success in sport is no reason to summon help from the Almighty, who must have more important things to do. Some dismiss it all as a sort of simplistic superstition or accept it as a pretty good psychological ploy that obviously works superbly well for me and therefore should not be knocked provided it is taken in a sporting context.

My own view is simple enough. The Almighty did not win those nine major championships for me. I did that for myself. Nothing is ever achieved in life without hard work and endeavour and I have served my time. I am quite sure the old saying is true that God helps those who help themselves. I am never quite sure about the idea of destiny. I sometimes think it is a reflective judgement; rather like being wise after the event. A simple example: I have always been regarded as an aggressive, almost heroic competitor who attacks and never plays safe when the whiff of victory is in my nostrils. That style of play was not God-given. It was the result of cold and hard calculation and it was backed up by hours of hard work. I realized early in my career that I had to shoot at the flags if I wanted to win tournaments. And yet it is an obvious fact that the flags, particularly in the final rounds, are always located near the sand traps guarding the greens. I therefore needed to aim at the flags in the knowledge that if I missed fractionally and finished in the sand, I could still save my par. That meant I had to become a trap player. I had to know there would never be any problem for me in sand and it followed that such confidence would allow me to be more aggressive in my approach play. So I practised and practised my bunker play until I could hole a few shots and play most of them as well as I would a long putt. It meant that while other guys who were inferior sand players would cut the ball or pull it away from the trap, I could go straight for the flag. That positive attitude won me nine major titles. Was that destiny or common sense? Who made it happen? Me? Or God? I like to think that God gave me the opportunity to do it. But I had to get on with the hard work to make it happen.

A man's faith is extremely personal, and indeed why he believes and how he came to it are sometimes as obscure as that which he believes. My faith is the most important aspect of my life; more important even than my family, whom I love dearly. I am not a religious man in the doctrinaire sense of the word. I do not subscribe to a particular faith. I am not tied by those special beliefs which separate one religious persuasion from another. I find all that very confusing, each of them declaring they have the truth which must be followed. That attitude has caused conflict, wars, terrorism and many deaths. My own faith is more basic. It is natural and uncomplicated and stems from the natural world I have seen and loved around me throughout my life.

Since boyhood I have had a passion for the great outdoors. Perhaps it was part of my elder brother Ian's influence. We were both suburban boys from Johannesburg, yet he became one of the fore-most wildlife conservationists in the world and I used my golfing fortune to buy land and breed horses. (In fact, while most young assistant professionals probably saved up to buy a car with their first wage packets, I bought a share in a delightful old horse with mine.) Ian came to believe that we were no longer aware of the value of the wilderness and he also believed that due to human ignorance we had lost our spiritual contact with the earth. I know what he meant. Not long ago, I flew to my stud farm in the great and desolate Karoo, the rugged semi-desert of the Cape Province. It is savage terrain but its climate and conditions are perfect to produce racehorses of stamina, strength and heart. One morning I rose just after dawn to be on my own. I went and sat by a lake at the foot of a small mountain. There are not many such moments of tranquillity in my life. It was a cool morning and suddenly the silence was shattered as a flock of geese tried to land on the water but were chased off by birds already there. The geese climbed, dived and tried again. But still the birds on the water refused to budge. It was a staggering ritual that was repeated several times until the invaders decided to move on. As they grew smaller in the distance, I looked at the nearby stream and the thorn bushes and the variety of trees and I realized that I could not comprehend the meaning and purpose of it all. In my mind I spoke to God.

I have an image of a force when I ponder on the nature of God. There is a dam near my farm and sometimes when the wind blows I walk across its wall and get scared as the water crashes against its sides. I try to comprehend what would happen if this wall burst, and then I realize the force of the oceans, of fire, whirlwinds, hurricanes and earthquakes. They are all minute compared with the force of God.

Now, I have to admit that any chap who has ever played against me and reads this will think it is a load of nonsense. He will say: 'I've played him. And he's ruthless!' And he would be absolutely correct, in one sense. I am utterly ruthless on the golf course. I am playing to win. When I go to the first tee I am getting into the ring. I am climbing through the ropes. There is no difference between me and a champion boxer. He has to land that one punch to knock out the other guy. I have to get round in one stroke fewer than the next guy to win the tournament. It is an awesome task – just one stroke's difference in 280 strokes. For me to do it means I have to summon up fierce determination to an intensity that sometimes frightens me when I think about it afterwards. There are times when I don't want to talk to anybody. I don't want to talk to my wife. I don't want to see my children. When I am on the golf course, I am transformed. In those moments, I can't have peace. When it is over, I can be myself again.

I am not, however, a pious man. I have never pretended to be. I have never prayed to win a golf tournament. I simply pray for the courage to keep going because I regard my life and golf as a mission; a daily choice between right and wrong decisions and actions. I meditate about twenty times a day. I begin in the morning when I shave. The first thing I do every day of my life as I rinse my razor under the tap is to count for seven seconds. It gives me just enough time to think about God, to let Him know I am aware and to ask for guidance.

There was a time in my life when I used a lot of bad language. Then I realized how futile it was and that it was evidence of a very limited vocabulary. So I stopped. I have never used bad language in front of my children. But now and again, without thinking, I slip back into my old ways and say something foul. Then I get the message. I have never been a drinker. In my days as a young professional I tried it once but became so ill that I never really bothered again. There is however another, more tragic, reason behind my abhorrence of drink. My step-mother was an alcoholic. My father remarried when I was a teenager and quickly I was aware that his new wife depended heavily on the bottle. She was a well-intentioned and kindly woman who always had my best interests at heart; but as a young lad I would watch sadly as dad carried her away from the dinner table and put her to bed because she was incapable of walking or staying awake. Her name was Dorrie and she drank brandy. The sad part of it all was that she was a very capable woman when sober and I got on well with her. But not when she was in drink. I never really found out what drove her to it. She had been divorced before she married my father and there was talk that she had never got over the break-up of that first marriage. Ironically, her daughter, my step-sister, who is now dead, also became an alcoholic. She once told me: 'Divorce is worse than death because it is rejection.' For Dorrie, who had two children of her own, it could not have been easy coming into our home and trying to take the place of our mother. It just doesn't always happen. Her drinking became a thorn in my side and when I got my first job as an assistant professional with Jock Verwey I left home and moved in with the Verwey family until Vivienne, their daughter, and I were married and found a place of our own. The experience with Dorrie made me realize that if I wanted a good family life and to be successful I had to lay off the liquor. I had seen the dangers and it was a great blessing because I had seen what alcohol abuse could do. Still, Dorrie remained devoted to my father and died a few years after him.

I think faith has given me another dimension to my sporting life; a perspective on all that I own. If I lost my business empire and my farms, I would still have my faith. I had it when I was poor and before I won anything. Maybe my faith helped me win. But there was never a plea to God to let me win or to let me make money. It all came about through complete dedication and being an abnormal person as far as work is concerned. I was happy before and I would be again. Of course, I would miss it all if it were taken away. I rank money as one of the four most important assets in life after my faith, my family and my health. There are those who will say this is a very cosy philosophy for a millionaire sportsman for whom nothing in life has ever gone seriously wrong. But how would he react in real adversity? How strong then, the faith?

My answer is that it has already withstood such tests. I have endured my share of hardship. I look back on the death of my mother when I was a child and the loneliness it brought. I think of the experience with Dorrie and her drink problem. I remember the time I broke my neck in a boyhood prank and had to wait a year to learn whether I would ever play golf again. And I remember, too, those years in the United States when my life was under threat from civil rights activists and I had to live with an armed guard. During that low period in my life I used to recite constantly Psalm 23, which begins: 'The Lord is my shepherd; therefore can I lack nothing.' But the passage that held particular significance for me goes:

Yea, though I walk through the shadow of the valley of death, I will fear no evil; for thou art with me; thy rod and thy staff comfort me.

Thou shalt prepare a table before me against them that trouble me; thou hast anointed my head with oil and my cup shall be full.

But thy loving-kindness and mercy shall follow me all the days of my life and I will dwell in the house of the Lord for ever.

For two years on the American golf tour I really did walk through the valley of death. But that prayer was of great comfort and saw me through. I knew I was not untouchable. I had no wish to die. But I also knew I had a moral obligation not to give in; not to run for home because people were making life difficult for me. I had no choice.

I knew the power and the strength of prayer and what it produced from within. So that day at Augusta, as the journalists smiled at my prayer, I let the moment pass without comment, even when somebody asked: 'Gary, did God have any message for your caddie?' They had, after all, been discussing the spiritual aspect of life. Missionary work of a sort. And at least it was a start.

CHAPTER 6
Vivienne

The first time I saw her, I decided I would marry her. I was fourteen years old and she was a year younger. Not that Vivienne learned of this teenage resolution until much later.

Of course, it helped that this vivacious girl played golf. Her father was the professional at the Virginia Park club where I played. Her brother Bobby was also an avid player. So it was that all three of us grew up together on the golf course. We competed fiercely against each other, invariably for money. Not much, of course: just a few coins in the kitty, and whoever broke 50 for nine holes scooped the lot. There were no concessions to Vivienne, except that she played from the Ladies' tees. This was serious stuff and she was just as determined to win as we two fellows and quite often did so.

Looking back I think she may well have recognized in those battles at Virginia Park some fire within me that made it quite clear how important this game was to me; how much it mattered for me to succeed at it. I came into their lives as a youngster who had not had the best of breaks in life, whose mother had died, who had seen his step-mother assailed by drink problems and who did not know much of the complete cosiness of a normal family life. Not quite a forlorn figure, of course, but self-questioning enough to need a sense of purpose that gave every task – even the most menial – an added dimension and significance as though there were always something more to be proved. It was an insight into my character that was to guide her throughout the rest of our lives together as Vivienne realized that my supreme fulfilment came through golf and the process of giving everything to win; not the acclaim and other benefits, but the sheer elation of proving to be the best.

In a way she probably sensed my destiny long before I did. And yet through all the triumphs and setbacks, the ever-changing patterns of our lives as we travelled the globe, met world leaders and other great men of influence, no longer had to worry about money and could afford the finer things in life, I do not think we have ever lost the sense of wonderment at it all that we shared right from the start. It is still a great adventure: one that began when we were teenagers, endured through the separations of tournament golf, the trials, tribulations and joys of parenthood and six children and eventually took us into grandparenthood and all the gratification of seeing our children carry on the values and standards by which we lived.

Behind every successful man there is a woman. Behind every successful champion golfer, there is a very exceptional woman, because whatever qualities of greatness and resolve it takes to lift one man above the rest, so too must they be found in the woman who shares his extraordinary way of life. I have already said that I sometimes think the real Big Three of tournament golf were Winnie Palmer, Vivienne Player and Barbara Nicklaus, because of the manner in which they accepted what was involved in accompanying their particular menfolk through life and the unquestioning sacrifices that would be involved in satisfying this burning ambition. I will not, for example, reveal which wife slept on a tiny camp bed in their Scottish hotel room so her husband could get a good night's sleep in what passed as a double bed. Nor the wife who bought numerous electric fans to provide her husband with a primitive form of air-conditioning in their hotel room. But these are the challenges that befall the wife of a professional who must give of his best every day.

And yet it really is a great adventure. Or rather, it must always seem so, otherwise there is no point to it. Arnold actually eloped with Winnie in the face of parental disapproval because it did not seem to them that this former paint salesman had much of a future, especially when he decided to turn his hand to professional golf. They lived in a trailer on tour in the early days because they could not afford motels. Whatever they achieved – and it was much – was always in what they saw as a partnership, even if Arnold was more visible because he hit the shots and won the titles in spectacular fashion.

Jack Nicklaus and Barbara were college sweethearts and though they never experienced the lean financial times, there were moments of crisis when each looked to the other for strength. In 1967, Barbara was taken ill in Las Vegas where Jack was leading the tournament with one round to play. He stayed at her hospital bedside until the crisis passed and then went out and won the tournament. Then, too, there was the time he looked to Barbara for strength when it seemed his career was in decline and probably at an end. She lifted his spirits and he went on to win another US Open and US Masters. Some time later, they were both sorely tested when one of their children was involved in a car accident back in the United States while Jack was playing in the British Open. He produced one of the worst scores of his career but never revealed the private anguish. Thankfully the boy made a full recovery.

From my own experience I know how important it is to feel that, win or lose, there is someone who really cares about you as a person and not necessarily for what you have achieved. It is for others to applaud and fête you when you win and understandably look to the new hero when he arrives. But there must be a sense of constancy to sustain you and it cannot be a coincidence that the marriages of the Big Three have prevailed over the rigours of these exceptional lives.

In general terms, it is easy enough to make a simple equation that golf is a protracted test of skills lasting four or five hours a day and therefore requires a rather controlled temperament to produce any kind of success at it. Such a person is unlikely to be volatile or erratic and therefore makes an ideal marital partner. And true enough, there was a time when the divorce rate among tournament professionals was extremely low; but I suspect that the increased incidence of break-ups – or, conversely, the more permanent relationships of my era – had more to do with the social and moral attitudes of the times themselves than with any common psychological profile.

What is difficult for the wife of a tournament golfer is the necessary acceptance that every day of their lives has, as it were, a tick or a cross by it. It is either success or failure depending on the score produced. He goes out in the morning to his work. If he comes back with a 70 or better, it has been a successful day. But an effort around the 80s is an obvious disaster which all must share. How many other businessmen – or married couples – face that kind of judgement and the personal questioning that goes with it on a day-to-day basis? More to the point, the touring professional can be literally out of work after two days if his scores are not good enough and he misses the halfway cut. The motel bill has to be paid, the luggage packed; and he – plus wife and kids – move on to the next stop to try again.

The life of a tour wife, then, is one of utter and unquestioning devotion. We were staying in a hotel in Jacksonville during a tournament a few years ago and were in the middle of breakfast when the wife of a young player walked in and sat down for coffee. She was waiting for his sports shirts to emerge from the hotel washing machine. He had already gone off to play. Whether he played well or poorly, he would not be back until he had practised, which meant it would be dinner-time before they met again. She remarked wryly that sometimes, if he suggested they turn in early in the evening – say 7 o'clock – he meant just that: he had an early starting time in the morning and needed a good night's sleep . . . So it is quite true that for all the domestic improvements that make family life on tour easier now – the crêches and the courtesy cars and the proper attention that is paid to the comfort of players' families – the ultimate sacrifice and tension remain the same as it did when Vivienne and I were taking our kids around the golf circuit. It is still a question of living on a knife-edge of performance every day; of at times being quite unapproachable in moments of desperation; of being cocooned in concentration yet still needing total support and understanding. Not an easy role for a woman to fulfil. In fact, quite an unreasonable duty to demand. There are times when I am so engrossed in happenings on the golf course that I do not want to speak to Vivienne. There are times when I have stared at her and not even seen her. She understands. We all accept the degree of other-worldliness that seems essential to this task. At Royal Lytham in 1974, I asked Jack Nicklaus what he had scored and he replied, rather surprised: 'I haven't even started yet!'

The fact that Vivienne knew from our teenage skirmishes at Virginia Park what was involved in trying to play the best golf did not make it any easier, but for certain I came to value and trust her opinion on matters relating to my golf swing. She had after all seen it in action longer than I had. If she noticed a flaw creeping in, then I listened to what she had to say and went to work on eradicating the problem straight away. She was a fine golfer in her own right, having reached two handicap. Moreover, she had watched me in action all over the world and always from outside the ropes among the ticket-buying public. Just a face in the crowd.

Essentially, golf is a solitary game in which you are competing against a great mass of rivals you cannot see while trying to control and contain your own imperfections. We all of us like to feel that somewhere in those faceless crowds on either side of the fairway there is someone who really cares – win or lose. That is why in the major championships the other Big Three have probably trodden as many fairways in our wake as Arnold, Jack and myself. That was the style Vivienne, Winnie and Barbara set, always carrying the seat-stick-cum-umbrella which has now become a sort of compulsory badge of office of players' wives on tour as they too follow their husbands stroke by stroke among the crowds. It is not an easy task. It means of course, that at times they hear the most hurtful abuse directed at their husbands by fans who have no idea who is standing within earshot. Mostly, they choose to ignore it, because no matter how difficult it is to bear, the customer has paid to come and watch and has a right to his opinion, no matter how ill-informed or badly expressed it may be.

It is one of the penalties of being married to a highly successful, high-profile golfer that a wife too has to move into the limelight as every aspect of the hero's life becomes the subject of public interest – not least of which are the woman he married, his children and his home. Some wives cope well. Certainly the Big Three set a magnificent example. Vivienne had a taste of public life as soon as I won my first Australian tournament in 1955 and told reporters I now had enough money for a honeymoon. The news was flashed back to South Africa and Vivienne found herself the target for photographers and reporters from numerous newspapers. Since then she has given countless newspaper and magazines interviews about the lifestyle of a globe-trotting wife and mother, because not even Winnie and Barbara travelled to the same degree as Vivienne in her determination to keep the family with me as much as possible. Moreover, her tastes and sense of interior design are of such exquisite standard that she is often asked by magazine editors whether they can photograph our home. On such matters Vivienne makes her own decisions. It can, however, be a precarious business when press are allowed across the threshold – or rather, allowed to make any contact away from the golf course. One very well-known player refuses to conduct any interviews at his home or allow his children to be photographed. There may be elements of personal security involved, but it is also important that children in their early years lead lives that are as normal as possible.

Barbara Nicklaus has an attractively independent streak and has managed very successfully to maintain this normal side to life for all the Nicklaus family – Jack included. A small example: every year she organizes an informal golf tournament for her friends and neighbours in Florida. They are all amateurs and it is a light-hearted affair. She asks Jack as a matter of routine if he will play but invariably he is busy. Not too long ago, he had a last-minute change of plan and informed Barbara that he was now free and could play in the guest day. She told him he was too late. All the places had been filled. The world's most successful golfer – whose daily appearance fee is quite impressive – had offered his services for free and had been turned down!

It was a delightfully refreshing episode which showed the fun and normality that even superstars can bring into their families once they are away from the spotlight. I do not think, though, that Vivienne, much as she knows and cares about my golf, would have dared to act in the way Toots Cotton did when she was convinced her husband Henry was playing with a putter that was not helping him; and more to the point, that her own lightweight putter was of more benefit. He disagreed. However, when the tournament started and he reached the first green and asked for the putter, the caddie could find only the lightweight version belonging to Toots. At the last moment, she had made the switch. Henry was furious and in his anger scored a 66. Even so, Toots made herself scarce after the round, though she felt she had won her point.

I am immensely thankful that Vivienne was present for most of my major triumphs and at my side to accept the acclaim. They were as much her triumphs as mine. She was there when it looked as though I had thrown away the 1959 British Open at Muirfield, and she screeched with delight when I hit the match-winning fairway wood close to the flag in the 1968 Open at Carnoustie.

And only Vivienne knew how close I was to quitting tournament golf in 1973 when my spirit was so low after major surgery earlier that year. Yet she knew I invariably produce my best when I seem to be beaten. She was sympathetic about my mood but knew me well enough to leave the decision to me. She knew full well I would bounce back; and of course a year later I won the British Open.

It is a matter of sadness that I have not always been present at the moments of her own great triumphs. To be frank, I have missed being present at the births of three of our six children, because the duties of golf obliged me to be somewhere else in the world; and at such moments I did wonder whether it was all worth it. I regret the absence for many reasons. I had missed a unique moment of life. I had not witnessed these little characters coming into the world. And perhaps equally importantly, I had not been there when Vivienne needed me; not there to hold a hand and encourage as she had been in my world.

We resolved that the inevitable separations that came our way, no matter how hurtful, would simply become part of our routine and that despite the distances involved, we would remain a close-knit family. All this was an essential attitude once the children were old enough to go to school so that neither they nor Vivienne could travel with me. Such separation is the curse of the travelling man and I remember Peter Thomson, an inveterate globe-trotter, saying that lots of families have to make that kind of emotional adjustment to separation all the time. Not that it makes life at the other end of the telephone any more bearable. I know that my children understand the dilemma that faces me – torn between home and international golf. They write me letters of encouragement which I keep with me and constantly read when I am travelling just to bring them all closer.

Another of Vivienne's great skills has been that while she can run the family single-handedly and efficiently while I've been away – taking all the decisions, whether large or small – she was always able to hand over the reins to me when I returned so that I did not feel like a visitor in my own home. A small point, perhaps: but vital in maintaining a semblance of balance in a life that has its extremes. In short, she has always been the sort of intrepid and inspiring person whose first reaction to any idea is 'Why not?', never 'Why?' Whatever the plan, it was all right by Vivienne. On one occasion we travelled with the children, a nurse and thirty-three pieces of luggage. Vivienne was in control and we never lost a single item – luggage or kids. Whenever we travel or are together at home, she always puts out my clothes for the day. It is her idea. To me – perhaps to both of us – there is a deeper significance and symbolism to this rather humble task. It is a simple demonstration of her care which has never wavered over the years. A gesture that, to her, I am still the important figure in her life.

She must have known all those years ago when she worked behind the counter in her father's pro shop that the little chap with the wide eyes saw her as more than just a partner on the golf course. He was offering her a job for life.

CHAPTER 7
The Man in Black

Everybody knew exactly where to find the new 1963 Natal Open champion when officials came to present him with the prize money and the trophy. He was waiting outside the clubhouse because he was a coloured man and therefore, under apartheid laws, prohibited from entering the building. And it was raining.

Sewsunker Sewgolum was a delightful man; a Cape Coloured of Indian extraction and a formidable golfer whose main point of interest to people outside South Africa was that he played cross-handed – the left hand below the right – and was, in my opinion, one of the best and most accurate players I have ever seen within 40 yards of the green. 'Papwa', as we all knew him, is now dead, but at the peak of his powers he played in Europe, winning the Dutch Open three times against high-calibre opposition, and was acccorded the respect and courtesy befitting a top-class sportsman wherever he played abroad. But when Papwa came back to the country of his birth, he had to revert to a sporting life of second-class status in which he needed official permission to compete each week against white golfers, for whom he was more than a playing match, because multi-racial contests were forbidden by law. How ironic that Papwa, the 1959, 1960 and 1964 Dutch Open champion, whose predecessors included Bobby Locke and Roberto de Vicenzo and who would be succeeded by such famous winners as Seve Ballesteros, Graham Marsh and José Maria Olazabal, was judged by standards other than his skill whenever he came home in triumph.

Our paths were to cross frequently throughout our careers; I came to count him as a friend and discreetly sponsored him on an Australian tour. In a curious way, too, I was to draw strength from his experience when later I was 'singled out' for hostile treatment for reasons other than my golf. It was an ironic role-reversal, in that my troubles started when I left South Africa and Papwa's occurred whenever he came back. In fact, the episode at the Natal Open was to give me the first chastening experience of just how the apartheid system of the South African government was to affect me personally for years to come in various parts of the world. In simple terms, I became an easy and obvious target for abuse, criticism – and sometimes much worse. I could not step off a plane without being held answerable for the apartheid system and all my protestations about sport and politics not mixing were brushed aside. So it came to pass that when Papwa was kept waiting in the rain for his prize, one newspaper attacked me viciously and demanded: 'Why didn't Gary Player protest at this kind of treatment?' There was a very simple answer. I knew nothing about the incident. I did not even play in the event. Not that it seemed to matter to the critics, who felt that anyway even a time-delayed protest from a player of my stature should have been recorded.

The trouble was that even when I expressed an opinion, I was still attacked. In 1965, when Papwa was told that he might not receive government permission to defend his Natal Open title, I was asked to comment and said that I preferred to stay out of politics but that I was disappointed that Papwa was not being allowed to play. Not good enough, according to some South African newspapers. It seemed I should have taken a stronger stand and that in some way I condoned the treatment that was being handed out to Papwa. This has been the pattern of my life and it was to become more than a battle of words.

Since those days, I have been the target of public demonstrations throughout the United States, in Australia and in Europe. At times, the threats and dangers were so serious that I had the protection of armed bodyguards both on and off the golf course. Wherever I played, I was regarded as a spokesman for apartheid – or at least the one tangible target its opponents could easily attack. The easy way out would have been for me to turn my back on my country and uproot my family to live somewhere else in the world. In fact, I was offered a million dollars by an American golf-club manufacturer to settle in the United States. In playing terms it would have made sense, because three of the four major titles of the world are played there and there were huge fortunes to be made. I often wonder how many more major titles I would have won had I set up home in the United States and eliminated the prodigious amount of travel I imposed on myself by constantly flying home. But in truth I had no choice. I am a man of Africa. It is in my blood. It is the most extraordinary country of wonderful people. A strange breed, aggressive but hospitable. I love the early mornings; to hear the bush dove, to see the lion, the elephant, the heat coming off the dry ground in the Karoo, and then the sunsets. There is an odour, a smell about it that is unmistakable whenever I get off a plane. It is my country. I could not give it up. I think of its spirited, heroic history. The great and noble African tribes – the marvellous and intricate black languages, traditions and rituals.

All of it is the Africa in which I grew up with my black friends. In those days I believed that it was presumptuous to assume that these great black tribes should be obliged to adopt our western ways at the risk of losing their own heritage and traditions. It led me to think about apartheid. We were told it offered a separate but equal way of life to all Africans of whatever creed or colour. And it seemed to satisfy my ideal. In fact, I went on record in 1965 avowing: 'I am of the South Africa of Verwoerd and apartheid.' The sad irony was that the way of life was certainly separate but far from equal. In fact, it seemed that the only reason for separation was to subjugate black Africans and keep them in an ignorance that was eventually to backfire on those apartheid policies.

My own views began to change, particularly as I travelled around the world. The injustice was so obvious and the implications quite chilling. If I am in a room with another man and I eat steak every night and just give him a slice of bread, he will take it for so long but then he wants his share of the good things. We've got to share. For me there has been no instantaneous Road to Damascus conversion but a growing awareness of what needed to be done. I am now quite convinced that I have subsequently played a significant role in trying to eradicate apartheid in my country. It is a terrible system.

I am also sure, however, that my personal realization and conversion was not influenced or accelerated by the anti-apartheid demonstrations aimed at me all around the world. If anything, they served only to harden my resolve not to give in to that kind of intimidation because what was happening to me was also a breach of the principles of civil rights. For two years in the United States my life itself was under threat. There were phone calls and warnings to police that I would be killed if I turned up to play. During the US Open at Merion in 1971, officials were so worried about the situation that I was given a round-the-clock armed police guard. At night three officers with guns kept watch inside the house in which I stayed and a police car patrolled outside in the street. The activists found the phone number of the house and kept ringing. I insisted on answering and said: 'My friend, what have I done to you? You are going to have to kill me because I intend to play in this tournament.' I refused to back down. When I practised and played I was accompanied by armed policemen. I was told that I could quit if I wished; but I refused, because I would not be beaten in this way. There was a certain injustice about it all, anyway. In those days when American involvement in the Vietnam War was a major issue, no protesters anywhere in the world ever took Jack Nicklaus and Arnold Palmer to task and asked them to answer for their country's action in the way I had to account for South Africa's actions.

Without doubt the worst anti-apartheid incident occurred in the American PGA championship at Dayton, Ohio, in 1969. It stands as a sad moment in the history of the professional game: protesters constantly tried to disrupt play and I am convinced cost me the title even though I played perhaps the most important round of golf in my life to lose by only one stroke. Oddly enough, the initial dispute with the civil rights activists did not involve me but centred on how the $200,000 profits from the championship would be distributed among the poor in that part of Ohio. There was also a demand for free tickets and this was turned down. However, Ed Carter, the tournament organizer, calculated that the protesters would plan to make maximum impact in Saturday's third round when the event was screened on coast-to-coast television.

More than 400 policemen were drafted in to break up any trouble as soon as it started. The problem was they had no idea where it would break out – until they realized that I was paired with Jack Nicklaus on the Saturday and we were both chasing the lead. We had been warned to expect trouble. We had also been told we could quit, but the thought never occurred to either of us. We did not have to wait long before the ordeal began: on the fourth tee, as I addressed the ball, a programme was lobbed over the heads of the crowd. It fell at my feet and I stepped away. It was removed and without comment I played my stroke. On the ninth green Jack was the target as he crouched over a birdie putt and in the stillness somebody shouted. He smiled and stepped away, but missed. Minutes later, as I walked in front of the clubhouse through the crowds to the tenth tee, somebody called my name. I turned. A cup of ice was thrown in my face. I was astounded. I gaped at this bearded man and said: 'What have I ever done to you?' He shouted: 'You're a damn racist!' Both Jack and I sensed that there must be worse to come and that we would not finish this round without further incident. He was worried because his wife Barbara and son Jack junior were in the crowd.

Then it happened. A black man broke free from the crowd around the tenth green and charged towards Jack, who raised his putter to defend himself. That was the signal for more trouble. Jack's ball, close enough for an eagle three, was picked up and thrown away. Mine was near enough for a birdie chance and was also thrown off the green. Then the police moved in and eleven people were arrested.

We stood around and realized it was time to resume play. Jack's ball was replaced but he missed his eagle putt. Some defiant streak within me made me hole mine for a birdie. Three holes later I was the target again when a ball was rolled between my feet as I was about to putt. Though we did not know it, that was to be the end of the disruption; but still the police were taking no chances and would not allow us to walk through the crowds to the press centre for our end-of-play conferences. Instead we were guided into the basement of the clubhouse to speak to the journalists. Jack was clearly shaken and said: 'Count me out of this championship. I was scared out there. But I don't even want to give these people the credit of attention by even talking about them.' I tried to make a joke of it by saying: 'It was like a game of gotchas out there. I stood over the ball and wondered who was going to grab me next. I am not looking forward to the final round.' But I had a serious message too and told the press: 'The majority of people were nice. I don't think you should let lousy things be published. If all the thousands of people out there are so nice, you can't let five or six drive you in. That's just letting them have their way.'

Did it take courage to come out and play the next day? Of course. But there was a tinge of indignation and determination there too. What was happening to me was wrong. I could only fight it. Otherwise I might as well pack up, go home and forget about world-class golf. Another thought, too ... I was within reach of yet another major title.

The next day I played under police escort. I was paired with Ray Floyd and our personal bodyguard marched with us, then surrounded every green, facing the crowd as we putted, looking for the first sign of trouble. This time there was none, although there was a touch of apprehension as I settled over every stroke. I lost by a shot, yet I was proud of the way I played and that I had not given in. Jack Nicklaus said he considered that it was probably the finest round of my life because of the strain involved. He also made me smile afterwards when I asked him if there had been any more trouble with demonstrators: 'No, just from a cop. He said he didn't like the look of the crowd to the left of one green. Could I therefore hit my approach to the right-hand side?'

Ten years later, I was still the target for demonstrators. This time it happened in Lyon during the French Open. I had learned long ago that it is pointless to argue my point of view with people who have no wish to listen. The protestors chained themselves to the main gate and threw down nails to puncture a few tyres. French Federation officials decided it would be wise to give me a bodyguard and even though there was no serious incident on the fairways, I was saddened that my wife and young family, who were travelling with me, had to experience the drama and tension of this darker side of my life. I was interviewed on French television and declared: 'I am not an ambassador for apartheid. Anyone who says that is just starting propaganda. I try to be an ambassador for good-will and love. I do not believe in apartheid in sports and I have done many things trying to show that.' Those demonstrators ought to have known, for example, that only three years earlier I had finan-ced a European tour for a young black African golfer named Vin-cent Tshabalala and he had captured the French Open championship at Le Touquet. I also asked Lee Elder, the highly talented black American golfer, to come to South Africa and play a series of exhi-bition matches with me.

My attitude was clear enough. The value of sport and the merit of winning must always be that everybody is allowed to compete. By that I mean that the only qualifying factor should be ability and I worked towards that goal in golf in South Africa. But it had to be achieved within the framework of the existing laws, no matter how unpopular or unjust they might seem, and this attitude was to find an echo many years later on the European Tour when various coun-tries began to ban South African golfers even though they were accredited members of the circuit. Tour officials took the pragmatic view that they could not contravene the laws of a country in which they played.

Even though we were able eventually to introduce multi-racial competition in professional golf, after many setbacks, the problem remained that the black golfers, including Vincent, found great dif-ficulty in raising the finance to compete. Many of them worked outside the game during the off-season to raise the cash to fund their competitive play: Vincent worked as a mechanic when not on tour. He still does. Some of us decided it would be timely to promote a series of blacks-only tournaments that would guarantee a complete share-out of prize money for these young players so that they could have the financial resources at least to start on the main South African circuit if they so wished. The idea was criticized by some people who thought I was being too liberal, or treacherous to white professionals, or at best trying to ingratiate myself with the black population. But I have long since given up trying to explain myself to those who have already made up their minds.

It was much the same when I became marginally involved in the notorious Information Scandal of the late seventies when it was discovered that public money was being diverted secretly by the Ministry of Information for propaganda purposes in an attempt to improve South Africa's international image. When the whole affair was uncovered by a public inquiry, it led to the resignation of the Minister, Connie Mulder, and in mid-1979 caused the downfall of Prime Minister Vorster who had to accept overall responsibility for whatever went on in his government while he was in charge. I think I played a large part in taking the lid off the whole business, because when rumours first began to circulate about various payments being made, everybody denied it; but when the television people asked me if I had been paid I admitted straight away that I had. It was one of the first pieces of hard evidence.

What happened was that I was approached by some government officials and asked whether I would entertain a few very important overseas businessmen by playing golf with them when they came to South Africa. It seemed harmless enough and nothing more than a good public relations exercise. When I looked at my diary I realized I had been offered an appearance fee of $50,000 to play in Australia that particular week. I am a professional athlete, so I told the government people I would not be able to play golf for them. They offered me a fee of R20,000 if I would change my plans and insisted it was very important for the future of South Africa so I agreed to play, even though their offer was not as much as I would have received in Australia. As I understood it, this was not a political operation. If they had told me it was to advance the cause of apart-heid then I would not have done it. But it was for the sake of future investment in the country and I have always seen myself as a patriot, though not always to whatever government was in power. I was quite open about the payment when asked because I am a profes-sional sportsman who gets paid for his time. I had nothing of which to be ashamed; but perhaps the shock waves of my marginal

A favourite study. As soon as I saw Vivienne I decided that we should marry — even though I was only fourteen at the time. She has been my greatest inspiration ever since.

'The best school in Africa'. That is my opinion and that was the task I set myself when we established the school I inherited as part of the Blair Atholl farm.

Our fame spread quickly. Even Glasgow Rangers football club sent a full strip for our first team who practise on the pitch adjacent to the school buildings.

I will not ask any of my farm workers to do a job that I would not carry out. Sometimes I prefer to get on with the job myself, like mixing cement with Willy Betha as we erect a new fence.

The masterpiece that emerged from a Florida swamp. The golf architect sometimes has to create his own landscape. I built high tees at Alaqua Country Club in Orlando to give the course more definition.

The creek by the 13th hole at Augusta where I thought my chances of winning the 1961 Masters had ended after I took seven strokes. Luckily Arnold Palmer made a crucial error on the last green.

The approach shot that finds the green deserves the chance of a birdie putt. One way is to produce flatter greens of even pace as here on Hilton Head National.

1990 FASHION REPORT

Golf World
INTERNATIONAL NEWS MAGAZINE OF GOLF • A GOLF DIGEST PUBLICATION • OCTOBER 19 1990

PLAYER CASHES IN

SPECIAL: GOLF CLUB BUYERS GUIDE: our biggest ever!

GOLF

Start of a new series by the game's masters

ALL I KNOW
by Gary Player

The world's best bunker player shares his secrets

EXCLUSIVE SURVEY Help shape the future of the game

LYNX LYNX LYNX LYNX LYNX

PLAY GOLF!

Clubs, the Game and How Best to Play It!

Special: Bob Drum On Golf Language

Gary Player's Remarkable Advice for "Grown-up" Golfers

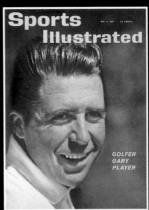

Sports Illustrated
MAY 2, 1961 25 CENTS

GOLFER GARY PLAYER

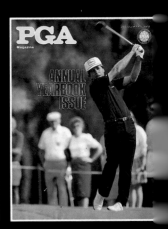

PGA
Magazine

ANNUAL YEARBOOK ISSUE

An exciting new South African magazine

GOLF NEWS
VOLUME 2 No. 2 FEBRUARY 1980 85c

The Golfer of the Year

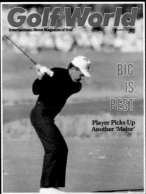

Golf World
International News Magazine of Golf

BIG IS BEST

Player Picks Up Another 'Major'

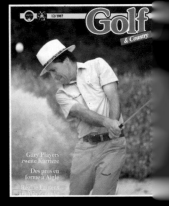

12/1987

Golf
& Country

Gary Players zweite Karriere

Des pros en forme à Aigle

The progress of a champion. My career as recorded by the golfing media

GOLF
ILLUSTRATED

FORTNIGHTLY
5th August 1988
£1.00

BUMPER TOURNAMENT REPORT ISSUE
Player pleases again to win the Volvo Seniors

PLUS
Scandinavian Open, Dutch Open, PGA Cup, US Women's Open, Bloor Classic and Hennessy

OPEN ROUND-UP
A look back, with more pictures from Lytham

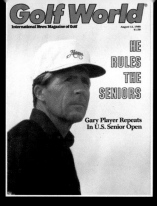

Golf World
International News Magazine of Golf
August 12, 1988
$3.00

HE
RULES
THE
SENIORS

Gary Player Repeats In U.S. Senior Open

The people's choice—Palmer for President
Sandy Lyle: My 2 tips to sink more putts

GOLF DIGEST

NEW SWING FOR MORE POWER

Gary Player shows you how to gain yardage at any age

Gary Player's MOD-swing swing

P G A
The Insider's View of Golf
April 1988
Three Dollars
Magazine

SENIORS CLASS
Not Over the Hill — High On the Mountain

Sports Illustrated

Hit it my way
by
GARY PLAYER

The USGA guide to the 1988 National Championships

Golf
INTERNATIONAL

FREE
JOIN GOLDEN POSTER

GARY PLAYER
AND TRAP STRATEGY AND OTHER STROKE SAVERS
CHRISTMAS GIFT GUIDE
WITHOUT GIVE AND WHERE TO GET IT
PLUS PETER ALLISS
ARNOLD PALMER
THE KEY TO BETTER GOLF
SEO LUCIEN O'LEARY
& WORLD WIDE RESULTS

BELLS SCOTCH WHISKY BELLS

golf world
newsweekly
August 3, 1972
60c

PGA PREVIEW:
PLAYER
DEFENDS
AT CANTERBURY

FLORIDA GOLFER
The Monthly Magazine For Florida Golfing
November 1989/$2.50

GARY PLAYER
Golfs Ambassador To The World

TIMACUAN IN ORLANDO

BRADENTONS PERIDIA

Man of Africa — an oil painting by John Meyer of a Gary Player the world does not often see. When I am off the golf course I wear my khaki around the farm, or on the site of a new golf course under design.

The beautiful gardens of Blair Atholl, and a moment of solitude to enjoy them. The 120-year-old English oak tree is in the background.

involvement revealed the scale of the secret strategy.

It dawned on me, inevitably, that a sportsman of my eminence in South Africa could not separate politics from sport for a variety of reasons, even if I wished. For a start, all South Africans – whatever colour or creed – were delighted when I scored victories overseas. My postbag and my reception all over the country proved that to me. It meant, with all due modesty, that even people outside my sport looked to me to take a lead because what they saw me accomplish was the result of honest and hard endeavour and therefore what I said and believed was unequivocal. Only occasionally, though, did I step into the political arena. I was so dismayed when the political right-winger Andries Treunicht ran for government office that I went on record saying that much as I loved South Africa, I would leave if he triumphed. Thankfully, neither event came to pass. And I was furious when Pik Botha, the Foreign Minister of the day, made a speech in which he actually blamed the United States for the violence in our country, and I declared: 'Our system is at fault. The only way is to give up apartheid.' My liberal views began to give me an anti-government image, but in truth I simply wanted the system changed. A little later I became very supportive of the views of Denis Worrall, the former South African ambassador in London who came back to contest the 1987 election, and I told the press: 'If we yearn for a democratic country where there is a place in the sun for everybody, then vote for Worrall.' And while he failed by only a few votes, the groundswell of public opinion subsequently began to bring about the changes for which we had all worked. It had taken some time, but it was happening, and for some reason I found myself thinking about an early experience in America's Deep South when I had just joined the American Tour.

I was paired with the black golfer Charlie Sifford, one of the most courageous and determined sportsmen I have ever met: he had endured hurtful prejudice in his own country and had prevailed against it. We were playing in Greensboro, North Carolina, which was then one of the strongholds of anti-black feeling. These people are boisterous at the best of times, but even I was taken aback at the way they treated Charlie. They screamed 'Go home, nigger!' as he played. They kicked his ball into the rough. Afterwards, when he came into the scorer's tent and we sat down to check our cards he jabbed his pencil angrily on the table and said: 'How can anybody play golf with this going on?' Yet he went out again the next day. He refused to be beaten, even though at times he was a very bitter man.

These days, of course, he is a stalwart of the Seniors Tour; but his example in those days helped me when I came under pressure against civil rights demonstrators on the US Tour. Like Charlie, all I wanted to do was play golf as best I could. That, too, is all we wanted for South African golf – that it be a question of skill, nothing else.

Charlie, in fact, made the breakthrough in American golf and others followed. Lee Elder made his own piece of history by being the first black professional to play in the US Masters at Augusta National in Georgia. I saw Lee as an inspiring character and asked our Prime Minister John Vorster whether I could invite him to play a series of matches, after which he would compete in various tournaments. It was of course a daring move to permit what was seen as multi-racial sport with mixed spectators as well. We were given approval and played before thousands of people of all colours without a hint of trouble at Huddle Park. They had come along to see two professionals at work. What Lee did was not too popular with some critics back in the United States yet between us we made a major contribution to bringing about integrated sport in South Africa. And I always felt that Lee should have received some kind of award – some official recognition – for the part he played in that process. He was surprised at the hostile reaction, as well as at the criticism he received at the time for what some regarded as merely a token gesture. But just to make the point that he had a genuine desire to compete in South Africa and that he would not be intimidated, Lee returned to play several events. Moreover, his wife Rose is a governor of the school that has been built on my farm for the children of the workers and local villagers.

Now cynics may say this is merely my attempt at insurance against further protest. In fact I know it is said that the only reason I have a black caddie is to forestall any kind of racist demonstrations at tournaments and that I always wear black clothing as some kind of symbolic gesture. In response I would mention first that I had a black caddie (called Smitty) on the US Tour in the mid-1960s and people still demonstrated against me. So that disproves the theory that a black caddie offers safe passage. But the other reason why this notion is so false is that I cannot afford to choose a caddie on the basis of his colour. I need the best caddie I can find to help me to win tournaments. True enough, Alfred Dyer – nicknamed Rabbit – is a black man and has worked for me for many years. But the fact of the matter is that he chose me. Before the World Series, the caddies put the names of competitors into a hat. He pulled out my name. I won the tournament and we have been a working partnership ever since. He is a friend and a travelling companion, but he would admit himself that he cannot choose the right club nor read the line of a putt. But then that is not what I expect from a caddie. I want him to be neat and punctual. One caddie I had was an absolute genius at club selection and lining up putts but I could never be sure he would turn up on the first tee, so he had to go. In recent times, I have launched a competition in South Africa for black caddies and I bring the winner to Europe each year to work with me. My objective is not to win favour but to improve standards. However, I realize that critics can put any interpretation they choose on my actions and there is simply nothing I can do about it.

As for the black clothing, I hate to disappoint the deep thinkers who were looking for some hidden meaning to it all. There is a simple and innocent explanation, and it goes back to my childhood days when I loved watching cowboy films. I imagined myself wearing the black stetson, shirt, jeans and boots with the silver spurs and the pearl-handled guns. Perhaps it was from these early influences that I acquired my love of horses and ranching which has never left me. Was there any national symbolism behind it? Perhaps, sub-consciously. If others see it as a personal acknowledgement that I come from the Dark Continent, then so be it. But it was coincidental and not intentional. What is true, however, is that my personal preference for wearing all-black clothing on the golf course became so well known that I was referred to as the Man in Black and the Black Knight of the Fairways because of my determined and aggressive style of play. We subsequently used the title to develop our corporate identity and trademark.

Not long ago I found myself thinking of another anti-apartheid episode that happened during the 1975 Australian Open in Sydney. It had been a bad experience for me. Peopled chanted 'Racist! Racist!' as I putted. They jumped over the fairway ropes to get to me. Somebody threw a bag of peanuts over my head as I putted and a day later a firework was thrown but did not explode. In all, about nine people were arrested in two days. But what I remember most vividly was a woman of mixed race confronting me with a baby in her arms and saying: 'This couldn't happen in your country, could it?' Her point clearly was that the races would never be allowed to mix in South Africa. I wish I could tell her this story of what happened recently in South Africa. There was a black woman who worked for my daughter Jennifer and who one day disappeared, leaving behind a little daughter for Jennifer to look after. This delightful little girl has become part of the family. She plays with my granddaughter every day. She comes to our house for Sunday lunch. My granddaughter does not look at her as somehow different. She is a friend. Both sit at the table. Both swim and get into the bath together. They see no difference in each other. That is how it must be when they grow up. That is the future.

In our country there are still monumental problems to overcome. The black man and the white man are both Africans and need each other. I take my hat off to President F. W. de Klerk because he has admitted: 'Yes. We were wrong. Yes, apartheid was wrong.' He has not just opened the door to change: he has, as they say, taken it off its hinges. I have become more vocal in my criticism of the system that has existed in South Africa. I have earned the right to make myself heard within the country because I have endured so much on its behalf beyond its shores. At times the name of Gary Player is to be found in the news pages raising doubts about the extremist views of a Pik Botha or Andries Treunicht. And my message is always the same. I see a country with a multi-racial government that will consist of all peoples and parties. Let them put their brains together to build a country where everybody has a place in the sun. And if I am accused of an about-turn in philosophies, my critics cannot have it both ways. The wind of change has at last reached South Africa and our country will be the better for it. It has touched me too. It was simply a matter of time, as it will be for others.

CHAPTER 8
A Crisis of Confidence

I was deeply troubled when I arrived in Troon for the 1973 British Open. It seemed my life had suddenly reached an unwanted and unwelcome crossroads. I suddenly became aware that I no longer wanted to play golf. I even felt I hated the game. Until that moment, the entire reason for my existence seemed to have been for the purpose of playing golf as best I could, and my successes brought me a sense of achievement and of purpose as well as a certain status and acclaim wherever I travelled. I was acknowledged as a superstar; but I was beginning to feel less like one.

Still, nobody could have guessed from my customary positive demeanour when I arrived in Scotland that year that I was enduring a savage inner turmoil. I remember thinking at the time that such a mood of depression was a sign of weakness and that I, with all my self-control and discipline, should be able to dismiss it. But the mood would not go away. Moreover, I was playing poorly and was plagued by a persistent and damaging hooked shot which only added to my misery. Only my wife Vivienne knew how I felt and, much as she loved me, she knew this was one problem that I had to sort out for myself.

I was thirty-eight, hardly the time for a mid-life crisis; yet I had been on the non-stop global grind for seventeen years, during which time no distance was too far to travel, no situation too difficult to bear in the pursuit of success. And it had worked superbly. I had achieved more than enough for one lifetime. I had earned my place in the record-books. I had the four Grand Slam titles to my credit, plus a string of other victories around the world. I had a delightful and loving family who wanted me to spend more time with them. I had enough money never to worry again. And I had my beloved horses waiting for me in South Africa. The irony was that golf itself was keeping me away from all of them, although I was certain this was not the reason for my disenchantment with the game that had given me so much. Yet it was an eerie feeling, as though I was taking a fresh look at my life and wondering whether the balance was correct.

By coincidence, about seven years later Jack Nicklaus was to go through a similar crisis in which he began to wonder about his way of life and found himself plagued by self-doubt. In fact the world's most successful golfer reached the point where he asked his wife Barbara: 'Tell me, am I really finished?' This was more than merely the constant ebb and flow of form that afflicts a golfer throughout his career for varying periods and which, by the day-to-day judgements the media imposes upon its heroes, can be magnified into a catastrophe that does not really exist. In the late sixties Jack had endured an extended period without a major win to such an extent that critics had written him off until he surprised them all by bouncing back to win the 1970 British Open in that play-off with Doug Sanders at St Andrews. The difference, however, was that during that earlier period of obscurity the only emotion was one of frustration at not being able to win again. What he experienced later was more a question from within about the purpose of it all. I knew how he felt.

Looking back, I can see that several factors conspired at that time of my life to burden my spirit and that the overall effect was to test sorely my approach to winning that had always been a demonstration of my confidence and zeal. Sure, there was an obvious skill involved; but a classic Gary Player triumph was always seen as the fulfilment of the little man's confidence over the brute strength of others. Thus, my confidence quota always had to be at a high level. But for almost a year up to that championship, it had been seeping away almost unnoticed until the events at Troon. I do not think I have ever reached a lower point in my life as I considered what would be involved in my decision to quit golf. An end to the career of course. No more championships – although even in this gloomy state, I still toyed with the golfer's constant hope that 'it will all be different tomorrow'. More to the point, a decision to quit meant there would be no more active combative involvement in the game I loved. Until then, it was all I knew. The fun at the top level is not just the winning of titles but being involved – actually scrapping with the best players while you too are at your best – to see who is the better man on the day. There is the bustle of the tournament, the people and characters around the game and the sheer commitment of being obliged to get on an aeroplane and go to places. For most of my life, that had been my concept of being active. To stop now, before I was forty, would be not so much a defeat as virtual exile from the life I knew and all the friends and rivals – the Palmers, the Nicklauses and the Trevinos – who were part of it.

I reflected on how I had come to this moment. During the previous year, I had felt a slight nagging pain in my side while I was playing golf on the United States Tour. Nothing much, really; when it persisted I consulted a doctor who diagnosed it as lumbago. At the end of the season, when I flew home to South Africa, the problem had still not resolved itself so I consulted my own physicians. They advised an immediate operation. They discovered that one of the urethrae, the tubes connecting the kidneys to the bladder, was blocked and had already caused some kidney damage which could only worsen if not rectified as quickly as possible. So at the beginning of 1973 I was admitted to hospital in Pretoria for the lengthy and intricate operation to rebuild the urethrae, performed by four of South Africa's top surgeons, Dr Hessa, Dr Venter, Dr Kloppers and Dr Schulenberg. Then the painful recovery process began. For the next nine days I was obliged to use a plastic bag strapped to my waist as a temporary drainage system. It was to cause me an embarrassing moment when I decided to walk round the wards and – being a well-known celebrity – try to cheer up the other patients. One lady screamed when she saw me. It was not adulation. I looked down at the transparent bag to see a rather unwholesome liquid and crept away, truly chastened. There was to be one unforgettable moment of bliss when I was reconnected, as it were, to 'mains drainage' and allowed to use the gents' toilets again. It was almost a ceremonial act that Sunday morning as I stood there and suddenly, as I felt at peace with the world, I heard church organ music. Truly this was heaven! I discovered that the hospital ward staff had to borrow the organ each week for their Sunday service because there were no funds to buy one of their own; so I decided that I would buy an organ for their permanent use in grateful thanks to the surgeons and staff and in memory of that sublime moment when all the world seemed right again.

Not quite. My golf game depends on constant daily practice. I have a swing that works best when it is worked hard and often. But now I was obliged to leave the clubs alone and wait impatiently for my body to mend. For a man who had been fit all his life and exuded strength and well-being as his trademarks, these were hard moments to bear. Worse still, there was endless time to dwell on the future. Was I finished as a world-class golfer? I knew exactly what it took to succeed at the very top; how talent was only part of the formula and how every aspect of a man was tested to the extreme on the way to victory. Some people say that experience is a dangerous thing because the memory of it punishes you. You know what can go wrong. And as I lay there in that hospital I was not sure I still had what it took to remain a dominant figure in the game. Nor would I know until I was allowed to start playing again.

I had undergone surgery in February and it was the best part of three months before my doctors allowed me to return to golf, which meant I had to miss the US Masters in April at Augusta and could only watch in envy and frustration as Tommy Aaron slipped past Peter Oosterhuis to earn the green jacket. As soon as I was given the medical all-clear, I rushed back to the US Tour and rejoined my rivals at Atlanta. The result was disastrous and with each poor showing my mood deepened. In seven events I earned a total of $12,000, whereas a year earlier I had been picking up that kind of money weekly. Yet more disturbing was that my hooked shot was becoming ruinous. I simply could not keep the ball on the fairway and, much worse, with that more powerful hooking action I was forcing the ball into deep trouble and giving myself the onerous task of fighting to save a score rather than producing a challenge.

I began to seek advice; everybody tried to help. Jack Nicklaus and Lee Trevino came along with their ideas, but nothing seemed to click with my consciousness, nor would the pieces fall into place. What I had failed to realize was that the process of recovery from major surgery can be lengthy and involves psychological as well as physical aspects. Even so, I was committed to certain events and so I turned up at the British Open that July in Troon, more in the line of duty than of winning intent. Of all the golf courses in the world, Troon is not the one on which to be erratic or to tackle with a violent hook. Part of my frustration in all of this was that I remembered how I used to play and how bad I had become. It was rather like a tennis player must feel as he watches shots pass him that in the old days he would have not only reached with ease but dismissed with match-winning returns. I was not, it seemed, the man I used to be.

That was when I confessed to Vivienne that perhaps my time as a world-class player was over; that what lay ahead was sheer punishment as I tried to recapture an ability that had gone and that I might become instead a rather sad figure, a has-been who refused to go away. I said: 'I feel like quitting. Perhaps it's time to go back home and concentrate on the horses and all the other things in my life.' Vivienne remained non-committal. I think she realized that for me to quit in those circumstances would be for the wrong motives. It would have been the worst defeat of my life and the most permanent. It would have been a decision taken, not because I wanted to be back among the horses more than anything else in the world but because I could not, as they say, 'cut it' in world golf anymore. All she actually said was: 'The decision is yours. Whatever you decide is all right by me. You will have my total support and loyalty whatever you choose.' It was totally reassuring and absolutely typical of the steadfast and unquestioning way she has helped me throughout my life since we were teenagers. But the problem remained; and it was still my decision.

Then a curious thing happened. By chance I happened to watch Christy O'Connor senior on the practice ground. He remains, with Sam Snead, the most naturally gifted golfer I have ever seen. He may have lacked a certain discipline and dedication but that only added to his charm and did not detract from his instinctive skills. I watched his casual effortless style and how he moved the club on the backswing so that the clubface was open at the top. I watched and studied. I never said a word and I am not sure Christy even realized how intently I scrutinized his method. I decided to copy it and went to work immediately with that old golfer's trick of 'thinking' you are someone else when you want to play a particular shot. Johnny Miller explained once that whenever he wanted to fade a golf ball with a left-to-right trajectory, he just 'thought' Lee Trevino and his particular action as he stood over the ball, and it worked. I 'thought' Christy O'Connor and in the last round of the Open I scored 69; too late to affect the outcome of the contest, won by Tom Weiskopf, but effective enough to give me hope.

I travelled home to South Africa in good heart and went to work on my farm in an attempt to restore my strength and energy while all the time working on the altered golf swing. Looking back, I cannot remember the exact sequence of events but suddenly I realized my swing and confidence were restored. I came home and told my father: 'Don't worry, Dad. It's come back. I am going to win again.' I was perky, brimming with confidence and impatient to play. In August I returned to the United States and instantly finished in the top ten. Then I won the Southern Open in Georgia during a run of form in which I was never out of the top ten in seven events. The old mood was back; but somehow I was even more determined to succeed, as though I were just a raw beginner trying to break through. In the autumn, I came to Wentworth for the World Matchplay championship and found my will-power and stamina tested to the limit during two confrontations – one with Johnny Miller in the semi-final, when he claimed I tried some time-wasting tactics on him as he waited to putt, and then in a marathon forty-hole final against Graham Marsh, when the tension affected both of us and we indulged in a minor squabble about teeing up within the markers.

No matter. I won the title for the fifth time and had come through the most critical period of my life, in which I had lost both form and confidence, yet revived to find new vigour and purpose to my life.

There has not been a great golfer yet who did not at some time have to endure a period of decline. When mine was over I realized that my experience had been part of the strengthening process. It had been a test of faith, too; another skirmish with adversity. But above all, it made me realize just how highly I valued the game and how important it was to me. To this day I do not think dear Christy knows what an impact he made on me and how in a way he unwittingly restored my swing, my self-confidence and my future in the game. A year later I enjoyed one of the best seasons of my career, winning both the US Masters and the British Open as well as the Australian Open. Moreover, there was another major – the US Masters – waiting for me in 1978. Don't ever write a champion off, no matter how lost the cause might seem. I know, because I have been there – and back.

CHAPTER 9
The Luckier I Get

Champions are abnormal people. It is not simply their talent which sets them apart: it is a compulsion to succeed and an obsession to pursue and perfect their skills for as long as they are able. To them, it is an unspoken duty. It entails sacrifice not only for themselves but for those around them, their wives, children and friends. In my case it has meant long separations from my family as I left South Africa to play golf around the world. The question has been asked of me: 'If your family is so important to you, why bother to leave home?' The logic behind that thought not only ignores the nature of my chosen profession (in that the great events are played outside my homeland) but also fails to consider the obligations of true ambition. For me, it was never enough to be the best in my country. My ambition was to become one of the best players in the history of the game. Initially it was a dream, but each success spurred that conviction and the desire for more. Of course I regret that I did not spend more time with my family and share with them their childhood, the teenage years and early adulthood. I know I gave them quality of time instead of quantity. But that has been my sacrifice; the time spent alone in pursuit of success when I could have been at home with them.

Consider the great champions of the game: Ben Hogan, Jack Nicklaus, Arnold Palmer, Lee Trevino. All of them were totally committed to their talent. They were obligated and had no choice. The profile of a champion is rather like a complex jigsaw puzzle. There are many pieces, and without all of them he is incomplete. Sound technique is only one of those pieces. Another is fitness. There has to be peace of mind, proper diet, patience, courage, an ability to enjoy the adversity of pressure, intelligent playing strategy and even the help of a good caddie. Perhaps most important of all, there must be this commitment to excellence.

The game is full of good players who never quite stepped into the class of greatness because they did not possess all the pieces of the puzzle. Tony Jacklin is a case in point. He did not fulfil the dream.

Britain was starved of a hero until he came along in the late sixties. I remember how the American professionals, as well as Bobby Locke, Peter Thomson and myself, came over before that and won the Open championship almost at will. Then Tony came on the scene in great charismatic style and within a year had won the British and US titles. It was a phenomenal moment in the history of the British game which had given the sport to the world and was now seen to be reasserting itself. But by the time Tony reached thirty, he was no longer a force on the championship scene. He had virtually packed it up. Many reasons have been put forward for this. Maybe he made too much money too quickly. Maybe he did not like travelling and being away from home. I refuse, however, to accept the feeble suggestion that he gave up trying to be the best golfer in the world because he realized just how good Jack Nicklaus really was and could never surpass him. After all, he beat Jack Nicklaus when he won the British and the American titles. Jack cannot win everything. I never considered myself inferior to Jack. It has always been my nature to strive to be the best. Why pick on Jack Nicklaus as an excuse for not carrying on?

The truth is that Tony was no ordinary golfer. Therefore he was committed to see how good he could become. If he had played rather nicely and won a few tournaments on his home circuit – like, say, that fine golfer Neil Coles – then it would have been his pre-rogative to play the game on those restricted terms. But I do not think Tony, with his talent, had that choice. So he will go down in history as a good player, but not a great one, although he has continued to contribute to European golf with his flamboyant leadership of the Ryder Cup team.

I do not subscribe to the theory that his confidence was so shattered by the way Lee Trevino beat him in the 1972 Open at Muirfield that he was never the same man again. And I flatly refuse to accept that Tony's career was ruined by a fluke chip shot and a piece of bad luck. Trevino did not beat him: Tony beat himself. Tony was short of the seventeenth green in two shots and took four more to get down. That was a cruel extravagance and the reason why he lost. He did not make his five. Yet a par-five had to be the worst that happened in that situation. When Trevino chipped in for his own five, Tony had paid a harsh price for his error. In any case, a great player bounces back from a bad loss. If you play golf at this level and get into those dramatic positions when the big prize is within reach, you soon realize what a nasty game golf can be. It really is a humbling game. You have to take your medicine because you are going to lose more than you win.

I was standing next to Seve Ballesteros when Tom Watson came over to congratulate him behind the last green at St Andrews in the 1984 Open championship. Seve had just stopped Tom's chance of a hat-trick of titles; Tom himself had fallen foul of the infamous Road Hole by hitting his approach clean through the green and on to the road. It was an irritating mistake and understandably he was disappointed with himself. But both Seve and I were astonished at the hurried and half-hearted handshake Tom offered the new champion. As he walked away Seve said to me: 'Look how that guy congratulated me!' If it had been Jack Nicklaus, the moment would have been totally different. Jack looks you in the eye and says: 'Well played. Well done.' You know he means it because he knows he will get you next time. That is the true attitude. You are going to lose a lot, so you had better learn to smile and enjoy the other man's success.

I am not always able to leave winning or losing, as it were, outside my front door. It still stays with me for a little while but I soon shake it off. That comes from experience and the acceptance that a missed putt can never be retrieved and might just as well have happened ten thousand years ago. It is the next stroke that matters. That thought has helped me win a lot of golf championships. Yet it is also a thought that must have haunted Greg Norman after his succession of near-misses in major championships. In his puzzle of success, there is a piece missing. I do not know what it is. I thought he would become the next Jack Nicklaus because he had it all – aggression, good looks and a fearless charismatic style. But there was something lacking. I do not believe that he lost all of those titles that were within his grasp because he backed off from pressure at the crucial moment. But clearly he was doing something wrong and needed to be honest with himself to discover it. It was not downright bad luck, either, because it happened too often. My attitude to good or bad fortune is summed up by that old remark of mine: 'The more I practise, the luckier I get!' Greg can look back on bad judgement and shot-making, not lack of moral fibre, when he considers the titles that got away. He has probably re-lived them all many times in his own mind. But they are worth considering, if only for the lessons they offer.

The 1986 American PGA championship was lost long before Bob Tway holed his bunker shot on the last green to defeat Greg by a stroke. Greg had played the last nine holes in forty strokes. That is where it all went wrong. Worse still, he had thrown away a glorious chance from the middle of the last fairway. He knew Tway was in the right-hand bunker and that he needed only a wedge to the final green. Clearly he had to put the ball close, not only to ensure his own par-four and possible birdie but to put the pressure on his rival who would then have been on the defensive, knowing he had to get up and down for par. This is the psychology of the big moment. But Greg threw it all away with an awful shot. He didn't even hit the green with a wedge in his hand and you can bet that as Bob Tway glanced at Greg's golf ball nestling in the tricky grass, he thought: 'Hell, maybe a four will win this!' Thus he was more relaxed as he played the recovery and the ball went into the hole.

Consider, too, the US Masters earlier that year when Greg needed a four on the last hole at Augusta to tie with Jack Nicklaus and force a play-off. Not only did he miss the green with his five-iron approach, but he put the ball wide of the right-hand bunker. If he is in the sand he has a chance of making his four. I know because I was in that bunker in 1961 and got up and down to win my first Masters. For Greg, that was not bad luck. He missed the last green with a five iron and did not deserve to win.

In the 1989 Masters he was playing such unbelievably good golf on the last day that he was looking at a possible 64 the way he was going. But then he stood on the last tee and reached for a one iron. Instantly he had changed his whole mode of play from one of attack to one of defence. Subconsciously, when he took that iron instead of his driver, he had told himself he would be happy to make a par-four. He had brought himself back to the level of his rivals and, worse still, he left the approach short of the green, chipped poorly and two-putted to lose even a chance of a place in the play-off with Nick Faldo and Scott Hoch.

It is easy enough to sit on the side and give an opinion – and hindsight, as I have said before, is an exact science. But I have been under that pressure many more times than he has. By contrast, in the British Open at Royal Troon later that year, I think he should have shown more caution and reached for the one iron. In the play-off, he was well aware that if he put the ball in one of those sand-traps he would have no chance of reaching the green. Wayne Grady hit first and Greg must have seen how close that tee shot finished to the traps, so that he knew a shot with his own driver would be taking a massive risk. In any case, a one iron from the tee would still have left him only a seven iron approach into the green. Instead he drove into the trap. That was bad course management; but I also believe he had lost the title before he reached that point. Earlier, on the short seventeenth, he hit a magnificent tee shot which just ran through the green to the back fringe. Then he chipped poorly and took two putts. It is not possible to make that sort of careless error and win major titles.

True enough, it was an outrageous 50-yard chip shot that Larry Mize sank on the eleventh green in 1987 which beat Greg in a play-off for the 1987 title, but it has to be remembered that Greg had lost the psychological edge before that shot was played. He knew Mize was wide of the green and therefore probably concluded that par would win the hole and the title. But he should have been determined to stick his approach close to the flag just in case Mize got down in a chip and putt. Instead he went for an 'anywhere-on-the-green' approach and with an eight iron left the ball 40 feet from the hole. That gave Mize the notion that par might halve the hole, and in that relaxed state ... down went the ball. Outrageous misfortune for Greg, but containing a lesson to be learned.

You can learn from mistakes, but you can never know what is going on inside a man. Nor can you say exactly who is going to become a champion. In my time, it was said that Bobby Cole, Tom Weiskopf and Hal Sutton – all men of enormous talent – would become great champions but somehow it did not happen. Some of the pieces of the puzzle were missing.

I like and admire Greg. He is an outstanding golfer. And he has followed on in my tradition of playing all round the world and establishing himself as a truly international star in Europe, Australia, the Far East and the United States. It would therefore be so unjust to his talent if he were not to win more major titles because it would mean in years to come that people might not know him. There are many obscure, short-term champions in the record-books. Yet Greg is better than them and deserves a higher place because he is such a good man for golf. But then, as my friend Jack Nicklaus says, golf was never meant to be a fair game. I suppose that goes for winning as well.

One man stands out in the new generation as possessing all the pieces that make up a champion. Nick Faldo shows relentless determination. He is driven by a compulsion to improve and sustained by that brutal honesty with himself that has to go with it. For him, his existing collection of titles is not enough. He wants more. That is the appetite of a great player. He is a rare example for younger players to follow and I admire the manner in which he dresses so smartly and elegantly when in public. I know how intense the fires of ambition can be and how single-minded a man must become to succeed. But Nick has now reached that elevated status where this pace must not be followed myopically at the expense of his image and obligations as a champion. His public sees him as a hero, not merely a good player. I am impressed at the way he practises to improve his skills so that whenever the public come to see him play, they are treated to a superlative display of effort even if the flamboyant aspect is at times limited.

Top-class tournament golf in the modern era, with all the wider opportunities offered to its top players as heroes, role models, advertising performers, columnists, authors, etc. has put a new interpretation on that old Walter Hagen axiom. 'The Haig', one of the most erratic but accomplished players of the twenties, would play a disastrous shot into trouble and then produced an astonishing recovery to save his score. He would explain that golf was a game not of 'How?' but of 'How many?' The task for the modern hero is that now both conditions have to be fulfilled. And sometimes it might seem the 'How?' is the more important qualification. It is a lesson we all have to learn – a duty that is part of the job of being a champion.

CHAPTER 10

The Lighter Side

A friend of mine was aghast when he received a phone call from one of our more lurid South African newspapers saying they were about to run a controversial exposé on one of his relatives. It was Christmas Day.

The reporter said: 'I'd like to call round with a photographer this morning and ask you a few questions. Take a few pictures of the family. It shouldn't take more than an hour or two.'

My friend was alarmed: 'An hour or two? Don't you realize it's Christmas Day? All the family is here and . . .'

'Is that particular relative there?'

'No, he damn well isn't. Look, I can't help you.'

'Don't worry, sir. A few questions will jog your memory. We're on our way. Perhaps you could tell your wife to delay cooking the Christmas dinner for a little while.'

'Look, I've told you I can't help you. I won't open the door.'

'See you in about half an hour, sir.'

By this time my friend was frantic and began to shout: 'There is no use coming. I can't help. Don't you understand? I cannot bloody well help.'

That was too much. The caller burst out laughing. My friend knew instantly he had been tricked. He also guessed the real identity of the so-called reporter. Gary Player was up to his old tricks. The practical joker had struck again.

The public sees me as a grim and determined character, a terribly intense and ruthless competitor – all of which is true. But I am a different person off-duty. It is as though the emotional aspect of my nature which sometimes lifts me to peaks of performance even I cannot explain, also has a daft – and at times irrational – side.

I cannot resist a jape. I was travelling in Zambia with Arnold Palmer and Mark McCormack and we booked into a safari lodge hotel where they were sharing a room. I knew Mark was nervous about wild animals and the great outdoors, so I crawled along the ledge outside his bedroom window, pressed my lips against the glass to make a grotesque face and than started grunting. Mark raced out of the shower, saw this creature at the window and shouted: 'Arnie! Arnie! Help!'

On another occasion I had gone on safari with some friends and we were playing cards in the evening. I wanted to go to bed but they insisted on carrying on into the night. What they did not know was that earlier I had found a dead snake and brought it back to the room. So there, in the darkened, smoke-filled room, I casually dropped it on the table. They scattered. So did the cards. I was left to tackle the snake.

When an old friend of mine came to visit me on my stud farm in the heart of the Karoo wilderness, I told him I would meet him at the railway station. In fact it is little more than a hut in the middle of the desert and looks more like a film set for a Western movie in its desolate location. The train pulled in and my friend got off. He was the only passenger to alight at the empty platform. The train then slowly moved off and he watched it recede into the far distance, leaving him to scratch his head and wonder what the heck he was doing on his own in the middle of nowhere. I was not to be seen. I had hidden my truck behind a fence and watched gleefully as the visitor searched the so-called station for a phone. No luck; not even electricity at this spot. So there he was, alone in the wilderness, no sign of life, no road and no idea when the next train might come through. I did not leave him in this plight for too long. Before the joke wore thin, I appeared around the corner of the building and greeted a very relieved friend: 'Welcome to Colesberg.' I am not sure he wanted to stay long.

Of course, the problem about being a practical joker is that you become a target yourself. I remember in the early days of the European Tour a young professional having to be very careful after the trick he played on his fellow golfers. This was in the days of the package tours around Europe and after one Spanish event he disguised his voice on the phone and informed the hotel that the players had to have their luggage packed and ready for collection outside their rooms at 3 o'clock in the morning and that they had to assemble in the lobby soon after to catch the bus to the airport. Everybody complied and dragged themselves from their beds in the middle of the night. The plane, in fact, was not due to leave until the afternoon! The culprit was soon discovered, however, because he made a simple and obvious mistake: he stayed in bed. He was a marked man thereafter on tour.

Some of the best practical jokes are the most harmless. A French professional was staying in one of the best hotels in Morocco during a pro-am tournament and returned to his hotel room one evening to discover that every piece of furniture – bed, chairs, curtains plus his luggage – had vanished. Even the door had gone from its hinges. He checked to make sure he was in the right room. There was no mistake. So he went down to hotel reception – even the phone in the room had gone – and said: 'Alors. My room has disappeared!' The manager assumed he had been indulging a little too much but was asked to see for himself. The Mystery of the Disappearing Room deepened. Where do the entire contents of a room go without trace? The pro had a suspicious thought. He checked with his amateur partners who were also staying in the hotel and immediately solved the case. They had stacked his furniture in their rooms.

I accept, of course, that the hoaxer must not complain when he is caught in the trap. I was on a fishing trip with my brother Ian in Mozambique and decided to take an afternoon nap. I had said to him: 'You know the only thing I don't like about coming here is the prospect of those enormous man-eating spiders.' I dozed off and awoke suddenly some time later with something brushing – crawling, so it seemed – across my face. I opened my eyes and there was this huge black creature with lots of legs on my face. I screeched and swiped it away. But it swung back. I hit it again but still it came back. Then I realized it was hanging from a piece of string. Ian had gone to the river bed and found a large dead crab. He tied a piece of string to it and then dangled it over my face until I woke up. That, I think, settled a few old scores as far as he was concerned.

What my father-in-law Jock Verwey did to me was not quite a practical joke but it threw me completely which I suppose comes to very much the same thing. He knows how meticulous I am about tidiness. If I see even a scrap of paper on my farm I have to pick it up and put it in my pocket until I find a bin. It is a habit that sometimes drives Jock crazy. On this particular day we were entertaining some influential overseas guests to cocktails on the patio of our home at Blair Atholl. Jock, who can be a droll, deadpan character, was there and knew that I was desperately keen for everything to go without a hitch. Listening intently to one of the more distinguished visitors, he suddenly picked up a banana from the fruit bowl, scoffed it and threw the skin on the floor. The VIP gaped. Jock carried on as if nothing had happened. I was horrified. Should I pick it up? Trouble was, that would draw everybody's attention to it. Should I leave it? But what if somebody slipped on it? I could just imagine the conversation later:

'Hey, you'll never guessed what happened to the ambassador at Gary Player's house. He slipped on a banana skin. We don't think it was deliberate!' Then I looked at Jock. He had an impish glint in his eye. And he smiled. The old rogue had deliberately set me up to see how I would react. I just collapsed with laughter at his cheek and the way I had been caught out.

Jock was my first teacher. He has also fulfilled many and varied other roles. He has been my colleague, boss, landlord, father-in-law, friend and mentor. He is the professional golfer I have known longest. He taught me to play golf, gave me my first job, even gave me a home for a while. I married his daughter and have always appreciated his help. I think he realized just how determined I was when he started to give me bunker lessons at Virginia Park club; pretty soon we were placing bets on nearest-the-flagstick and I was taking the money. I was only fifteen at the time and he had been South African Matchplay champion three times. His capacity for work is phenomenal and his reputation as a teacher kept him in huge demand even when he should have been taking life easy. After all, as a teacher he had produced some fairly successful pupils. Quite apart from my own efforts, he taught Vivienne how to play and she became a two-handicapper and won many tournaments. Moreover, his son Bobby became a US Tour regular for a while as well as a successful campaigner in Europe and South Africa with a string of successes to his name. Long after Jock should have retired, he insisted on running his own driving range in Johannesburg and giving golf lessons. He explained: 'If you sit down you are finished. Doing things – being in demand – that's what keeps me young.'

I am an unashamed giggler. And once I start I find it difficult to stop. I am also a big cry-baby. In the United States one evening I went to see the award-winning film *Out of Africa* which was based on the story of Karen Blixen and the adventurer Denys Finch-Hatton in Kenya and starred Meryl Streep and Robert Redford. As soon as I saw the sights of Africa on the screen I felt homesick and began to blink back the tears. I was grateful that I was sitting in the dark and that nobody could see me crying. Later that week, I took Vivienne to see the film and said beforehand: 'I cried when I saw it. But this time there will be no problem because I know what to expect. Anyway, it is only a film.' As soon as the film began, the tears welled up again. I looked across at Vivienne. She was crying too!

The value of a sense of humour is that it represents a sense of perspective in life and an ability not to take everything too seriously all the time. I know, for example, that I am probably the only golfer in the world who has a catchphrase or motto that symbolizes attitudes that have become associated with me. Quite a few in fact. When I told a journalist: 'Don't write me off!' it became a sort of battle-cry that typified the Player style of golf. And there was the time I spun round on a spectator who said I was lucky to hole a bunker shot and said: 'Yes, the more I practise, the luckier I get.' That, too, became a Player catchphrase, though it also summed up a serious philosophy.

I know, too, that my accent is often mimicked; so are my constantly positive attitudes on almost every subject. Yes, I admit it is absolutely true that after playing in the Nations Cup one year at Dalmahoy on the outskirts of Edinburgh, I told the press: 'These are the finest flagsticks I have ever seen anywhere in the world!' It was a serious point, because they gave such excellent definition for judgement of distances. But to the waiting press I think there was a feeling that this was the power of Player's positive thinking going a little over the top.

I would make one other observation on this. I have always seen my role in golf as that of a performer. Of course what I do is skilful, but it is based on drama and excitement. I disagree with the view that the golf course is an office and that I am doing such a serious job I have no time to be an entertainer. I think it is true that Palmer, Player, Nicklaus and Trevino are all from that school of thought that accepted that the game's heroes had to be larger than life, and it may well be the reason why, as we have grown older, the Seniors Tour has had such a great impact, while our younger counterparts at times struggle for an identity the public cannot find.

In terms of positive thinking, I will never allow myself to dislike a golf course because that defeats the object of the exercise. Instead, I tell myself that this is an opportunity to excel. Everybody else, for example, might say how bad the greens are, but my view is that nobody is holding a gun to their heads and demanding that they play. Moreover, the prize money is there to be won and somebody is going to take it. Admittedly it did take me some time to come to terms with the demands of the Old Course at St Andrews and I said some critical things about it. But I was not the first golfer ever to need time to learn the art of St Andrews. Bobby Jones actually tore up his card on the first occasion he played it. Before he had even finished play, he threw the pieces into the sea.

Somebody once asked me seriously whether I employed a gag-writer for some of my more quoted quips. I took it as a compliment but nothing could be further from the truth. The *mots juste* just happen on the spur of the moment. I remember playing a practice round with Jack Nicklaus before the 1968 Open at Carnoustie when he teed up on the last hole and hooked out of bounds. He put another ball on a peg and did it again. He teed up a third time and just kept the ball in play by a few inches. I shook my head sympathetically and said: 'Don't worry about those first two, Jack. That's the best you could have done from that lie!' And when I won the 1974 Open and used a one iron from the tee most of the time instead of taking a driver, I said that club was the most important thing in my life. More important than my wife, someone asked? I thought, then smiled: 'Well, of course if it comes down to a choice between my wife and the one iron . . . I'd miss her!'

I cannot claim to have been the first man to observe that golf is a humbling game, although it is a classic example of the wisdom I think is to be found in well-turned phrases. For that reason, I am an avid and constant reader of the Book of Proverbs as well as the quotations of famous men whose knowledge comes across in this way.

It is a far cry from the family-speak we have at home. I suppose every family has this kind of crazy dialogue which is special and intimate to them yet quite meaningless to anybody else outside who overhears it. For instance, even though my daughter Michele is a grown woman and much-travelled executive in the fashion industry she is still called 'Squiddles' in our house because of the time we were staying at Gleneagles Hotel when she was a tiny tot and saw a grey squirrel but could not pronounce the word! My delightful grandson Roberto is only two. His father, my son-in-law, is of Italian extraction and with my daughter Jennifer he runs a highly successful restaurant in Johannesburg so young Roberto has acquired the continental touch. One day when he discovered a horde of sweets I keep for the children in a drawer of my desk he declared: 'Ooh la! la!' That is now our constant family greeting. It is the family catchphrase.

I think a parent has a different way of communicating with each child; a different wavelength that each understands and makes each of them feel rather special. Amanda, our youngest daughter, has a nonsense nickname. I call her 'Cookalooks': it means nothing. As a matter of fact I call my grandson 'Zookalooks' and my granddaughter 'Snookalooks'.

I suppose a sense of humour is God-given. It cannot be acquired, and yet it is supremely important, particularly in moments of crisis. I still recall that day in the PGA championship at Dayton, Ohio, when my life had been threatened and a demonstrator broke through to tell me the threats had nothing to do with my being a South African. For a second I saw the funny side of it all and said: 'Is that supposed to make me feel better about it?' I think even he smiled.

CHAPTER 11
He's My Brother

It was almost time to sign the contract and buy my first ranch when the owners asked for one final condition of the sale. Would I promise to retain their faithful black foreman and look after him? They were so insistent that I was intrigued and impressed by their determination to secure a future for this employee. It occurred to me afterwards that perhaps if I had refused they might have declined to sell the place I was to call Bellerive, in memory of the venue of my 1965 US Open win. Truly, therefore, this must be a remarkable man. I agreed to take him on and in so doing struck up one of the closest and most enduring friendships of my life. That was twenty-six years ago and Willie Betha is still working with us at our Blair Atholl farm. He is without question one of the most impressive men I have ever met in my life. He never went to school, yet he has a wisdom of life and a knowledge of the African ways upon which I draw avidly. What exists between us is an unspoken respect for the other man's strengths.

There is a curious parallel here with my brother Ian's experience during his lifetime as a conservationist in which, among other achievements, he received rightful international acclaim for saving the white rhino species from extinction. Very early in his career as a game warden he met a wise old Zulu called Magqubu Ntombela who had spent his life in the Umfolozi Game Reserve and was to become Ian's closest friend and mentor. They worked tirelessly to save the rhino from the poachers and killers and eventually transported four animals to Kruger National Park where the herd began to breed again without threat of slaughter. Laurens van der Post, the distinguished explorer and philosopher who has played such an influential role in shaping the attitudes of Prince Charles towards the environment, paid a unique tribute to my brother when he declared: 'Ian Player is one of the outstanding conservationists of our time and has received almost all the major awards in the world.' That list of honours includes the Gold Medal for Conservation from the San Diego Zoological Society as well as the Prince Bernhard of the Netherlands Knight of the Order of the Golden Ark. When Ian was honoured in New York for his work, he took Magqubu with him and, though this proud Zulu had never travelled so far in his life and could speak no English, he talked about his life and times in front of a distinguished gathering of environmentalists while Ian translated, and received a standing ovation when he finished.

Both men saw their wider role as that of making more people aware of the value of the wilderness. To this end, Ian had established the International Wilderness Leadership Foundation in 1974 to raise funds for the training of local people as well as the purchase of equipment for game rangers. To this day he and Magqubu remain partners as they take small, selected groups of people on safari in the Umfolozi Game Reserve to see and experience the wilderness at first hand, sleeping in the open, or occasionally in tents, and trekking sometimes four miles a day. Ian believes in the value of silence so that the sounds of the African bush can be absorbed. He and his party will sit round a campfire at night just listening to the distant roar of a lion, the grunt of rhino or the shriek of a hyena. It is a most fulfilling moment and seems to emphasize the words of Laurens van der Post: 'This is the highest task of man, to preserve the continuity of creation.'

In practical terms, this was a bond of purpose that united Ian and Magqubu; and in a different way Willie and I found ourselves unwittingly launched on a path that has earned each of us the other's respect and trust, a path that has never wavered and that was to have wider benefits. It began in a simple way with a common interest. We both revelled in the sheer exhilaration of hard manual labour and together once built a huge stone wall at my farm. It took us two weeks of dawn-to-dusk work, mixing cement and lifting stone, but we did it. We plant trees and hoist sacks of grain, irrespective of the weather, and toil around the farm rather like workmates anxious to get the job done well and quickly. It is, of course, the penalty of having a constant time-limit on every aspect in my life as another task awaits. We are both aware of this factor and that soon I will have to move on somewhere else. In these moments of sadness, Willie says: 'You must be a man. It is your job to travel. You know what you have to do.'

His loyalty to me is beyond question. When I sold that first ranch, on which he had worked since he was six, he agreed to move to my new stud farm at Colesberg. This was a man who I doubt had travelled more than twenty miles anywhere in his life before that moment. But he journeyed 700 miles to live and work in the rugged Karoo region of the Cape. We built a brand-new block of houses for Willie and the rest of the workers and their families on the ranch and Willie ensured that they were always kept in perfect condition. His home was best of all, its garden filled with various vegetables.

Eventually he came back to live and work at Blair Atholl. I have introduced him to some of the modern ways and even taken him on an air trip. But when we settled in our seats, he declared: 'We are too heavy. We cannot fly.' He remains unconvinced about some other modern inventions too: when I won a tournament in the United States, one of my office staff told Willie he could fax a message of congratulations to me. He wrote on a piece of paper which was duly pushed into the machine and emerged when the transmission was complete. Willie was told I had received the message on the other side of the world. He shook his head and said: 'No, Mr Player cannot have received that piece of paper. It has just come back out of the machine! Try again.'

Whenever I return from an overseas trip, Willie is one of the first to greet me at the large iron gates to our estate; but then he is already aware of my homecoming because the flight path for incoming aircraft takes them over our farm. He says: 'When I see the big aeroplane, I am happy that it is bringing you home.'

He has a fierce pride in his work. It is almost a vocation to him and he will not tolerate slackers among the work-force. He is scrupulously tidy and expects others to be so. What he made me realize was that the true relationship between boss and worker is really a partnership; one cannot function without the other. At Blair Atholl, it has been one of my primary ambitions to maintain a happy work-force. We meet every Wednesday for our *indaba*, a general get-together in which all aspects of our lives are discussed – theirs, mine and those of the managers. They have free homes, no water bills, no hospital bills. If they want various items, for their homes or for work, then we talk about it and get the matter resolved. We also voice our opinions about the way the work is being done, and this might mean that I have to tell some of them that they are not pulling their weight and that things had better improve. Willie will make sure that it does. But they also have their say. The important aspect of this system is that ill feelings are not allowed to fester and everybody knows exactly where they stand. I will say: 'What is your problem? What is it about me that worries you? Tell me. I will tell you what is worrying me about you. You are arriving fifteen minutes late for work. You are not picking up the bits of paper.'

Such is the range of topics covered in these meetings that they can go on for two hours. No matter how intense the discussion, the *indaba* always closes with a prayer.

When I bought Blair Atholl, just outside Johannesburg, it was both as a family home and as a spelling ranch for schooling young Thoroughbred horses until they were two years old and able to race. This was where they learned to take the saddle, to canter round the track, to become accustomed to the starting stalls so that none of it would come as a serious shock to them when they went into proper training. Moreover, it was an ideal spot just outside the city at which to show young horses to potential buyers who otherwise would have to make that long 700-mile trek south to the remote stud farm at Colesberg to see them.

Blair Atholl stood on 1,000 acres and was formerly the home of one of the best Jersey herds in South Africa. The water flows through the estate at four different levels and in the garden there is a huge 120-year-old English oak tree, rather similar in size to the famous one outside Sunningdale clubhouse, or the other that dwarfs the Augusta National building. The house has been re-designed in a Spanish style and inevitably I have built practice tees, a putting green and a bunker adjacent to a small lake just down from the house. It is not stocked with fish because I am not a serious fisherman – unlike Jack Nicklaus. When he made his first visit to South Africa and came to our farm at Magoebaskloof, we stocked a lake with trout and even fed them mincemeat so that they grew quickly enough before he arrived. Personally I find more satisfaction in planting trees and shrubs, because I see them as part of the environmental legacy for generations to come. When we arrived I looked at all the trees that had been planted on Blair Atholl by the lady who previously owned it and realized how far-sighted she had been; and how selfless, in a way, because she was making provision for a beauty she knew she would never live to see. Other generations would look at the trees and be grateful for the joy she left behind.

When I took over, I found I had inherited a school for the children of the workers and from the surrounding villages. There were 120 of them and I discovered that the teacher was compelled to turn away more than sixty prospective pupils a year because there was no room for them. I resolved that we had to build a school big enough to take them all – and as many more as wanted to come. It may have been regarded as a case of charity beginning at home, but I did not see it as such. Like Ian, I was looking to the future. Like the previous owner of Blair Atholl I saw that there was a contribution to be made even though I might not see it come to fruition.

Throughout my career, I have received an average of about 300 requests every month for money or other assistance from people all over the world. Invariably after I have won a tournament, the volume increases. It becomes known, for example, that I have won something like R500,000 in the RJR Championship and people assume I can afford to buy a little minibus for their congregation or some other item for a worthy cause. Most are also well aware of the well-documented account of how I gave away my US Open winner's cheque in 1965 to cancer research and junior golf in memory of my mother Muriel who died of cancer and that I continue to contribute to that charity around the world. What was needed at Blair Atholl, though, was not charity but a way forward. We all knew that education would be the biggest need of the day in post-apartheid South Africa so that we could play a more significant role in the world's affairs. Yet we were being hampered by a high illiteracy rate.

I took my son Marc to one side and said: 'We have a responsibility to educate the kids in our area. And not just the children of the people who work for us. I mean for the community as a whole – whites as well as blacks. Instead of giving out all these bits and pieces, let's concentrate on that task. Let's build one of the best schools in Africa.' Thus we established the Gary Player Foundation, through which we would filter all such work. The constitution of the Foundation aims to promote physical as well as educational well being. We approached all the sponsors with whom I was involved, especially those in the United States, and asked them to donate sums towards the project. More than this, we made it part of the deal in various cases that they would donate a sum of money each year to the project. Most of them readily agreed. Pretty soon, the money began to come in, but we were still left to find the lion's share and have contributed at least 80 per cent of the cost of the school buildings. Even so, it was a proud day when the school was opened and Lee Elder's wife, Rose, agreed to become trustee. (Lee and I had played the first significant multi-racial golf in South Africa during an exhibition match in 1973, as I described earlier. A year later, there were fifty black golfers competing in the South African Open.)

We now have two schools and they stand only few hundred yards from my home. There is a nursery school for 120 children and a primary school for 280 pupils. We even received recognition from the Glasgow Rangers Football Club, who sent our school first team a complete set of blue shirts, socks and shorts. There is accommodation for the teachers and their families. Each bungalow has two-and-a-half bedrooms, a bathroom, living-room and kitchen. Most of the teachers are married with grown-up families, so they are extremely experienced in education. We also have approval for our project from the African National Congress. Whatever money comes into the Foundation is primarily for education, although it saddens me at times to see how other funds left for educational purposes by multi-national companies who pulled out because of anti-apartheid pressure have been misspent. It is a shame to see that there has been such poor control of their use. For our part, we simply carry on in our own quiet way, although I sometimes think that if we had just a tiny percentage of the $60 million that is reputed to be available each year in South Africa for charitable work, we would be able to expand and develop other ideas we have.

One of the most joyful moments of my year comes on Christmas Day at Blair Atholl when all the farmworkers and their families – perhaps as many as 300 – assemble on our lawn in the morning, sing songs and exchange gifts with all my family. Good fun, of course, but it also holds a deeper significance for me. It is a demonstration of how we regard each other and that what lies behind all our festivities is a genuine respect and warmth, not contrived but quite typical of our daily routine.

My regret is that I am not fluent in a black language in the way my brother Ian has become. My father could speak three black languages and I think in modern South Africa it is important for such languages to be taught compulsorily in schools. Forget about Latin: let our children speak the rich and varied languages of their own land, apart from Afrikaans and English. It is, after all, the fundamental way in which understanding can be reached; and it is the only way forward. It is a preparation for the future which has to be achieved in the present. That is the lesson that Ian and Magqubu, Willie and myself have learned. It has guided our lives.

CHAPTER 12
No Pain, No Gain

It causes slight consternation whenever I inform the air stewardess I would like to sleep on the floor throughout the overnight flight and will not bother with the rare wines, the rich food or the movie. It must seem such a waste of travelling first class. But then, it is much the same routine in whatever luxury hotel I stay around the world. I much prefer the floor to the bed – though I would never dream of asking for a reduction in the room rate for not using all the facilities! Such episodes invariably are regarded as offering more evidence – along with the bananas, the raisins, the mealie meal maize, the punishing daily exercise routine – that I really am a fitness fanatic.

There was a time, twenty years ago, when my fellow professionals smiled at my antics and dismissed me as some kind of crank. These days the same men are to be seen every day in the fitness caravan on the USA Seniors Tour desperately doing the exercises in an attempt to reduce the size of their stomachs and regain some fitness. The more pressing reason now is that there is a lot of money to be made on the over-fifties circuit; indeed, more than many of us made in in our regular tour careers. But what these professionals came to realize rather late in their lives is that tournament golf is an athletic pursuit, not merely a cross-country stroll.

I have to admit that the secret of my longevity, not just as a successful player but also in terms of personal fitness, was not the result of some blinding prescience in my youth but was caused rather by a series of apparently unconnected happenings that combined to direct me towards the fitness path. From my boyhood days, I knew I had to work hard to keep up with the other guys, who were all bigger than me. My brother Ian was brutally blunt about it and told me that I would always be small so that I had better compensate by improving my strength and stamina. I could only have been fourteen years old when he took me on a mile run and I stopped halfway, absolutely shattered and exhausted. I told him I could not take another step. He actually kicked my backside and I carried on to finish. That was my first lesson about effort and determination. He was deliberately hard on me, as though he sensed what lay ahead. There was a pear tree in the front garden of our home in Johannesburg. He tied a rope to the branch and made me climb, arms-only, as high as I could. Eventually, after days and days of trying, I reached the top. Another lesson about the value of endeavour. Curiously enough, I went back to our old neighbourhood years later. The house had gone but the old pear tree still stood there.

In those early days, however, the physical emphasis was not so much on fitness, other than that which came naturally from playing first-team rugby and cricket for King Edward VII School, but more on the exuberance of achievement – climbing trees, jumping from great heights and other daft and youthful escapades. It was one such stunt that broke my neck. I was fifteen years old and a gang of us began jumping into a compost pit of dried leaves and grass. Of course, I just had to be that little bit better – a touch more spectacular – than the rest so I performed an excellent swallow dive head first into what I thought would be a soft landing area. From that height, I hit the bottom. The impact knocked me out, and when I regained consciousness, I discovered my neck was fractured. It was to be a year before I could even think of playing golf again and the doctor told me there was a point when it seemed questionable whether I would ever walk again.

That enforced absence from the game seemed to instil a sense of urgency into my life and for the next two years I practised and played every day. While I pursued some remedial fitness work, I had not even then come to realize the importance of the overall physical condition in sport. That perception did not really strike me forcibly until I played in the US Masters for the first time and found that I could not reach any of the par-fives in two shots while Arnold Palmer, Jack Nicklaus and company appeared to achieve the task with ease. That is when I knew I had to be stronger to match these fellows on a stroke-for-stroke basis. Accordingly, I embarked on a weight-training programme (helped enormously by Roy Hilligen, a former world title-holder), and followed it scrupulously, even though people warned me it would harm my golf by making me too muscle-bound. That simply was not true, because by doing exercise I was also improving my blood circulation and in any case my golf swing and other exercises kept me supple.

The night before the final round of the 1965 US Open in St Louis, I went weight-training. I weighed 165lbs, yet I was lifting 325lb by the squat method. Quite apart from the strength involved, that achievement gave me an immense sense of confidence as I faced Kel Nagle, a man much older than myself, later in the play-off.

Since those early days on the US Tour, several items of weight-training equipment have become essential items in my luggage, even if they do cost me excess baggage charges. I invariably carry another 60lb in weights in addition to my golf clubs and clothing. Even now I try as far as possible to ask the tournament sponsors to install a bicycle machine and some weights in my hotel room for use during my stay. Most times they are happy to comply, but if there are problems I bring my own kit.

At the age of fifty-five, my daily fitness routine lasts for an hour. If I am at home, I will complete it first thing in the morning and look forward to the prospect. But when I am playing in tournaments, it is the last thing I do at night and there are times when it can be an intensely difficult task. The routine may have to be performed after I have endured a long day in which I will have practised, played, then given a press conference plus television and radio interviews, signed autographs, put in my post-match practice and probably attended an official dinner before returning to the hotel sometimes after midnight. And yet what I realized long ago is that the pursuit of this routine at times when I did not feel like doing it was producing more than physical benefits, because I was imposing a fierce self-discipline on myself that would sustain me when I was under pressure in a tournament. We are born with a degree of determination, but the rest has to be cultivated. So by doing all these things – building the discipline, the strength of mind to accept adversity, working hard to a point almost of punishing myself – I was developing self-control. I suspect pressure is self-imposed anyway. Stand there and let thought and mind run away and suddenly the out-of-bounds becomes more important than the prospect of hitting the ball in the middle of the fairway. Think about missing a putt and it will happen.

There is no question that the most important quality that has helped me to win more than 157 tournaments in my career was this strength of mind. That truly was the difference. Tom Weiskopf once criticized me for my technique and I told him later: 'Look, this isn't a beauty contest. It's getting the ball into the hole that matters.' That is the meaning of will-power and it has to be exercised all the time and in various ways. That also is an essential benefit of my daily routine, even at this time in my life. I begin with 30 minutes of work on the bicycle machine. Then I do an average of 300 half sit-ups because they are tougher on the stomach than the full version. I use my wrist roller – a 4lb weight which is attached by rope to a bar which I wind up to improve my wrist and forearm strength. I also perform one-legged squats and a lot of lower back stretching as well as reverse back arches, because the golf swing puts massive strain on the lower back. The number of back sufferers in world golf is quite staggering and most medical experts are now of the opinion that the danger of the golf swing is that in fact it exposes weaknesses that already exist in the back – which is why it is essential for younger golfers to follow a strict strengthening regime early in their careers. That said, the list of famous back sufferers includes Lee Trevino, who needed back surgery to fuse the spinal discs together; Seve Ballesteros, who hangs upside down on a trapeze device to separate the discs and ease the pain; and even Jack Nicklaus, who was forced out of one US Masters with back trouble and once confessed: 'In recent years there have been nagging pains in my back.'

I vary my fitness routine. It may sound silly, but I like to surprise my body. Or rather, I do not want it to know what I am thinking. Putting it in simple terms, I might do a series of forty sit-ups then switch to a set of ninety just so that my body does not become accustomed to a regular pattern. In a way, it is as though I am coach and trainer to my own body; as if there is some sort of partnership between the two of us. This kind of 'other-person' attitude is quite common in golf as a player castigates or encourages himself as thought talking to somebody else: 'Gary, why did you do that? Come on, you know you can beat him!'

From my schooldays, I knew that the fitter the team, the better it played, and therefore the more successful it could become. In consequence I regarded golf as an athletic pursuit while most of my contemporaries revelled in the minimal physical demand they felt it imposed on them and argued that the swing itself was the best exercise for the game and that a hectic nocturnal social life was no serious handicap (that is, provided everybody else followed it too). However, when a group of British professionals were tested at a human performance laboratory in London, scientists were staggered at their poor state of fitness. Very few could touch their toes and the respiratory and heart responses after strenuous exercise were, according to the report, 'no better than the man in the street', which suggested to me that golfers were still excusing themselves from the high obligations of athleticism.

What I realized was that I had to be in supreme physical condition to give myself any chance of success in a tournament; and in my case that also meant overcoming the vagaries of jet travel – and whatever havoc they cause to the sleep and digestive processes – as well as combating tiredness or heat or cold or whatever else I might find wherever the aeroplane deposited me. Thus I discovered the importance of the floor in both aeroplane and bedroom, not only because of the obvious consistency but equally importantly for the firmness provided by both to help my back. Of course there are other tricks to ease long-distance travel when boarding an aircraft, the most important of which is to to try immediately to 'get on the clock' of the eventual destination. I know some travellers who alter their watches to the new time as soon as they board the plane. For me, this means instant sleep and I am fortunate in being able to nod off with ease. I forgo the meats, the wines and the heavy foods and other delights of first-class travel but instead eat a lot of fruit and salads and gulp down considerable draughts of water. Even though at times I am not that thirsty, I keep pouring it down because long-haul jet travel five miles up in the sky dehydrates the system. I take Vitamin B, found in wheatgerm, wholegrains, nuts, etc., because it improves mental sharpness and helps the nervous and digestive system. I also take Vitamin C – citrus fruits, etc. – because all body cells depend on it. I even take garlic as a blood cleanser. When I get off the plane I take a hot bath followed by a cold shower just to stimulate my blood circulation. I am then 'on the clock' and treat it as a normal day no matter how tired I am. I might even have one cup of coffee to keep me going even though I dislike caffeine. Equally important is my intake of mealie meal, a kind of maize from Africa which mixes with water to a porridge and provides essential roughage and regularity (absolutely vital for somebody like myself who could be obliged to play at any time of the day and then spend up to five hours on a golf course before obtaining relief).

What I am trying to achieve as quickly as possible is that fine balance between the right state of mind and perfect fitness that will allow me to play as I know I can. I often recount two pages from my diary just before I arrived for the British Open at St Andrews in 1978. It started in Johannesburg when I was up at dawn to watch my horses in training and then had three business meetings followed by a television commercial and press conference before boarding a plane for London. The flight took fifteen hours; I then had to attend and address a meeting in London, fly by helicopter to a golf club for an exhibition match, then catch an overnight train to Scotland to start practice for the championship. It was just part of the old routine.

I am not, however, a bionic man. The Player machine is subject to occasional wear and tear and breakdowns like the kidney problems that occurred during 1972 and required surgery. But whatever physical problems have presented themselves since that time can be considered part of the Player ageing process – including a prostate difficulty which had become rather embarrassing because of the length of time I would wait in expectation in the locker-room while my colleagues came and went with consummate ease. It required an operation for me to return to normal service. But it was worth it. I wear contact lenses, but only when I play golf – to sharpen my sight for the longer shots. I have no need of them in everyday use.

In any catalogue of bad habits, I never had any problems about smoking because after my first experiment with a pipe, my mouth felt like the bottom of a bird cage. I threw the pipe away. And one serious attempt at heavy drinking was all I needed to cure me for ever. I had gone to New Zealand with David Thomas, Harold Henning and Peter Thomson; we had played twenty-six challenge matches in thirty days, and on the last night I declared: 'I am going to get so drunk I will have to crawl out of here.' I insisted the drinks kept on coming and ordered David Thomas to mix the strongest he could imagine. He obliged with whisky/gin/vodka cocktails which I just gulped down and asked for more. They carried me out. The next day, I felt like death. Maybe worse. I vomited in the hotel room. I went to the chemist for a cure and was sick in the shop. I was even sick on the aeroplane. Another lesson: if you abuse your body, you pay the price. Never again.

In modern times there has been a complete re-think about physical fitness for golf and some professionals on the Regular Tour admit that without a daily work-out in the Tour gym, they would not be able to get round the golf course. Certainly physical fitness routines have extended the careers of senior players.

From all of this, a physical profile of the ideal golfer could emerge. As a matter of fact, I think it already exists. Take a look at Popeye, the Walt Disney cartoon character. He is the ideal specimen. A thin neck makes it easier to turn on the backswing; no big shoulders, but a strong pair of biceps and forearms; a narrow waist and powerful backside, thighs and legs. In fact, the ideal build would be the bottom half of Jack Nicklaus with the top half of Arnold Palmer. Certainly if other sports have produced an ideal build – and that is certainly the case in basketball, high-jumping, sprinting etc. – then golf itself will define its own ideal profile. Yet even the perfect specimen will still have to follow a punishing daily routine.

I did it all by trial and error. The newer generation has more scientific knowledge available. But it still comes down to hard work. I have to admit that while the most unpleasant aspect of my life was the way I had to keep leaving my family to play overseas, the most difficult aspect has been to do my exercises five times a week. Sometimes there would be a strong temptation to put them off until tomorrow. But the old cliché is true: it never comes. And anyway, there was more at stake than just fitness. I had to show that body of mine who was in control. Perhaps I always will.

CHAPTER 13
My Kingdom for a Horse

My love of the horse began in childhood and it has never left me. Its simple origins can probably be traced to all those Western movies that enchanted me in the early years. But what developed as I grew to manhood was an abiding passion. Even now, I can still recall the mixture of exhilaration and fear as I clambered upon a horse for the first time in my life and then felt the great animal begin to break from a walk into a canter and then into a gallop. I was nine years old.

It happened that soon after my mother died, a schoolboy chum Frank Hodgkinson and his parents invited me to spend the weekend on their farm just outside Johannesburg. My father came from farming stock but this was to be the suburban boy's first taste of rural life. It was a magical world of massive fields and fences and horses and barns and chickens and cattle. It was the world of the cowboy. And I knew I belonged. So it came to pass that I hoisted myself into the saddle. Frank was an accomplished rider and what should have been a sedate stroll developed into a classic chase out of the Wild West. As soon as we were far enough away from the farm house and adult eyes, we began to race. The horses responded and we began to gallop across a maize field. I bounced out of the saddle, lost the reins but grabbed the mane. I slid all round that horse's neck. I lost the race – but I did not come off. I was a horseman.

Looking back, I now realize I had an instinctive feeling for the horse that went beyond those schoolboy celluloid dreams. It came to me that day: the smell of the perspiration, the whole atmosphere. Taking the horses back to the stables, washing them down, walking them and getting all the perspiration off. That unmistakably was when I acquired the taste. By the time I was seventeen and had turned professional, I joined forces with my boss Jock Verwey and bought a delightful horse called Judy. I think she cost me most of my first wage packets. In my spare time I used to ride her round the golf course, then groom her and feed her with loving attention.

Before that, my only other connection with the equine world came from selling programmes at the Turffontein race track to make a bit of pocket money while I was still at school. These days I sometimes go back to that track in my capacity as an owner and breeder and, as I mix with the great racing figures in the game, I reflect on that boy selling programmes.

Even when I was still toiling for the breakthrough in golf, I knew that one day I wanted a farm of my own in South Africa and whatever else it produced, there would have to be plenty of horses. That ambition was realized when I bought Bellerive, a 900-acre ranch at Magoebaskloof, several hundred miles north of Johannesburg. It was a great farm and the region can best be described as the Switzerland of South Africa, high in the mountains with lots of pine forests and mist and damp. The dams were filled with trout and it was an idyllic place from which we exported timber all over the world. Sure enough, I kept a few riding horses which seemed to satisfy that boyhood obsession. There seemed no serious ambition to do more. That is, not until I was invited by a Texas rancher during a tournament to visit his spread. That was when I beheld the famous Quarter Horse for the first time. It is an incredible animal. It is so-called because it is the fastest horse over a quarter-mile sprint. It is stocky – like a Mr Universe. It is built with great muscle, as opposed to a miler which is sleek, thin and athletic. With this animal, you could pull logs. The Quarter Horse is very much a real worker on a ranch and is used to control the herds of cattle. It is brave and instinctive and has a tremendous turn of speed in short bursts which enables it to keep the cows in order. The rancher said to me: 'You just sit in the saddle and hold on. It will do the rest.' And so it did. As the cows came into the paddock and tried to get by, the horse ran this way and that. It skidded. It turned. I sat there as this animal kept them all in check. It was a sensational feeling. A bit like being on a rocking horse, because I was not in control. But there was more to my delight than simply the characteristics of this great horse. I found myself in love with the complete atmosphere: the cowboy boots, the belts, the buckles. That boyhood dream had been reaffirmed.

With customary Player zest and commitment, I resolved to take some Quarter Horses back to South Africa where the breed was unknown. I reasoned that they were so versatile they simply had to be highly popular – on trail rides and for farm work. Indeed, I could foresee that every kind of rider – men, women and children – would become devoted to the Quarter Horse. I brought over sixty-six Quarter Horses at a cost, I think, of about $300,000. Mark McCormack said he thought I was crazy but conceded that if this diversion helped me to recharge the batteries for greater success on the golf course then it was really a sound and wise investment. But that was not the reason I bought them. This was not therapy. I wanted the breed to become popular and succeed in South Africa. What I had not fully realized was there was no chance of showing off the ability of the Quarter Horse there because there were no races in which it could compete, nor much chance that the Thoroughbred clubs would allow the animal to race. It soon became clear that the Quarter Horse venture was not going to be a viable proposition. I was not making money – indeed, it was costing me money. Eventually I sold them. A man took all of them except one off my hands: that one I kept for my personal use. And as I reflected on the lessons of that project, I concluded that the only way to make money in horses was by breeding and selling Thoroughbred racehorses.

If this had all started as a romantic notion from boyhood, then the economics of the horse business were beginning to make me realize that there was much to be learned and many more mistakes to be made, unless they could be avoided. I knew that my farm in the mountains was not the ideal place to breed Thoroughbreds because of its damp climate and hilly terrain. So I asked some experts to carry out a survey and find for me the ideal place to breed horses in South Africa. It took them five years; eventually, they came up with Colesberg, or rather, the wide open spaces of the Karoo region of Cape Province. I had asked them to take water samples and they discovered there was the ideal blend of calcium and phosphorus – so essential for building strong bones – to be found in the streams and lakes. The climate, too, was perfect. Hot summers to keep the horses fluid and mobile and cold winters to kill off the ticks and the likelihood of any other diseases or ailments. Moreover, there was as much land as the eye could see where a horse could run and run to build its stamina and strength and to learn the sheer exuberance of the gallop.

While this search had been going on, I had bought my first Thoroughbred. He was called Prussian Pride, a marvellous runner and a tremendous athlete. I bought him from a trainer after his tendons broke down. But I was still in the learning process because in truth he was not the kind of horse that would make a good stallion. Even so, I set out with him and a few mares. It was an amateurish start; but at least it was a beginning. In any case, I still had my golf career to follow and I decided that wherever possible I would combine the two interests. After all, the game took me all over the world, so I would use the travelling time to study horses from books and, depending on where I found myself, I would visit stud farms to talk to horse breeders and try to learn more.

So on those long intercontinental flights I devoted time to the study of bloodlines, paid attention to the genetics and even listened to tapes on all aspects of breeding and horsemanship. I went to Newmarket, met the experts and questioned them. I watched all the great races. I travelled to Thoroughbred farms throughout America and slowly my knowledge began to grow. I learned what to look for in a good horse; what qualities it should reveal and how judgement at times is virtually instinctive and not necessarily dependent on a scrupulous study of bloodlines and breeding.

There was, however, another aspect to all this endeavour. I wanted a life outside golf for a variety of reasons. I looked at my dear friend Arnold Palmer, for example, and realized that he liked nothing better than to take a week off and go and play golf with his buddies at his home in Latrobe, Pennsylvania, or at his Bay Hill club in Florida. Nothing wrong with that. Yet I suspect he might have endured longer as a champion if he had found a consuming interest away from golf that would also have given him a perspective on the sport and allowed him to come back refreshed and keen after even the shortest interlude. To be honest, I no longer have the time nor the inclination for that kind of casual golf. There are too many other things to be done, and in any case playing golf has to mean something for me to be able to give of my best. Moreover, there is always the nagging thought at the back of every sportsman's mind about what would happen to him if everything suddenly went wrong and the career was over. The fact is that I wanted another career just in case this should happen. It meant, of course, that all this study of the bloodlines of great horses was of great therapeutic value because I could forget about golf when away from it – even between rounds – yet returned each day ready and full of vigour to play again.

There were, however, more mistakes to be made. As soon as we moved to Colesberg and its 4,000 acres, I got into the Numbers Game. I learned afterwards that nearly everybody falls for it when they move into the Thoroughbred breeding business. It is almost a disease. You become obsessed with the quantity of horses you breed in the hope that amid such volume there is more likely to be a gem – a

Secretariat or a Northern Dancer – that will make it all worth while in terms of effort and finance. At one stage I had close on 250 horses – brood mares, foals, yearlings, stallions, horses in training and two-year-olds. It was far too many. I had to win to break even and I was using my prize money from tournament golf to finance the horse business.

I dreamed, like every breeder, of producing the great horse. As I discovered, it was possible to define the conformation of an ideal horse. The length of neck, the proportion of the hind quarter to the rest of the leg, a good backside for power, and overall balance. But then, there is something else: an indefinable but recognizable quality that has a parallel in golf. The man with the perfect-looking swing does not always make a champion, while the player with the most wicked-looking action often prevails. A young horse may have shocking looks but turn out well. Is it heart? Or courage? Or spirit? Or intelligence? Whatever it is, it marks the difference between winners and losers – be they horses or golfers.

I found I could accept the whole ethos of horse racing because of its similarity to golf. The best performers cannot – and do not – win every time. In fact, even the most successful golfers must spend about 90 per cent of their time losing – and by that I mean not coming first. And this acknowledgement breeds a certain acceptance of adversity and a deeper appreciation of success when it comes.

The first time I saw Colesberg I knew it was a marvellous place. It ranks with The Curragh in Ireland or Newmarket in England or Lexington in America as one of the world's great centres for Thoroughbred horses. They can roam far and wide in the Karoo. They learn to run, learn to be strong. In Colesberg the paddocks measure 500 acres and there are plenty of them, so that a horse is never restricted. A lot of breeders live in this remote community where most of the telephone lines are shared between several farms and sometimes it can take a lengthy wait to make a call because maybe a couple of farmers' wives are exchanging recipes or chatting the morning away. Colesberg has its own little golf club in the desert where the so-called greens have to be coated in oil and constantly rolled to keep them flat. On a Saturday afternoon the farmers turn up to play and their wives bake them milk tart and sometimes carrot cake for tea in the tiny clubhouse. When I am amongst these men I love the talk of horses, the gossip, the stories of some of the tricks that have been tried and failed, the tips, the word on new ideas and all else that goes with the game. There is always a tale to be told – of the horse that was sold for a lot of money but turned out not to be the Thoroughbred it should have been; or of the mare that missed her expensive appointment with the stallion because the lorry broke down *en route!*

It is an extraordinary aspect of the horse business that everybody in it really cares. There is never any indifference. It is pure passion in which the well-being of the horse is paramount and all else is secondary. Truly, the commitment of those involved can never be doubted. There can be some cruel setbacks at times, as hopes are dashed when a horse dies or goes lame or a foal is born with little chance of survival. In those moments, it is no use raging against bad luck or ill fortune. If what happened is nobody's fault, then the matter must be closed and forgotten. But then it is a game of contradictions anyway. The philosophy in breeding is simple enough: 'Put the best with the best – then hope for the best.' It does not always work out like that. Secretariat, for example, was my all-time hero. He could be running last but then he would lap the field. He had such courage, besides his phenomenal ability. He was an American national hero; he was even honoured by the Mayor of New York. When I saw him run I said to myself: 'One day I would love to own a son of Secretariat.' A dream of course; but one day it became a reality. I owned one of his sons. True, there were some similarities with his sire, but my horse turned out to be a very ordinary stallion. Yet there was no point in getting angry that my great plan had gone wrong.

What I realized was that there could be no certainty of success through owning a huge stock of horses; that the numbers game was not the best way. It was another lesson well learned. I had about fifty brood mares at Colesberg and a decent mare could cost me $100,000. The smart method was to concentrate on quality and limit the number of horses to, say, twenty-five with the very best bloodlines. In a sense this is the third phase in the career of Gary Player, horse breeder. Moreover, I discovered that while Colesberg is an outstanding breeding ground, it remains rather inaccessible to potential buyers. Johannesburg is the acknowledged market-place, and that is where the horses have to be shown.

My estate at Blair Atholl may be small in comparison to Colesberg but at least I have the chance to become more directly involved in the horse breeding business at my home farm. The problem with Colesberg is that I rarely visit it more than twice a year, because of my other commitments. And I find I want more satisfaction than simply reading all the information from the farm – the good news and the bad – from a faxed message in whatever hotel I find myself wherever in the world.

There is the challenge, of course, of finding the right formula for a champion. You find perhaps an out-and-out stayer that runs forever but just does not have any speed. So you take a stallion that has a burst of speed and you inject that speed. Maybe you have another mare with a stocky neck. All her foals come out small and stocky. So you send her to a stallion with a slender, long-reined neck, a tall horse with long legs to get a bit of balance. It still has a lot to do with the eye, even though you have to study the bloodlines. You are trying to breed the perfect conformation of horse. When they are twenty months old, it is too early to say what kind of horse they will be. But if they look the part – very strong, a beautiful shape and very athletic – they have a chance. And if, just if, you have a horse running in a major race, it is thrilling to think that you have bred it, might even own it and that, quite apart from the prize money, there are bonuses through the breeding system and that you will also benefit from stud fees thereafter. It is as engrossing as any bet on the horse.

Seve Ballesteros once said to me: 'My friend, why are you so interested in horses? There's no money in horses.' I said: 'Seve, if you win the US Masters and I win the Kentucky Derby, there is no comparison in how much more money I will collect over the years.' He could not believe it. Another personal bonus is that the wonders of modern communication make it possible to keep in touch wherever I find myself in the world. One of my horses was running in South Africa; I was in California. I set the alarm for four o'clock in the morning, phoned the commentary service in Johannesburg and listened to the race. My horse won. But at that time in the morning there was nobody I could tell. I have even been travelling by car in Florida and pulled in to the side to listen on the carphone to a race in South Africa; and at one time I was flying at 33,000 feet in a Gulf Stream executive jet when I phoned my office in Cleveland to learn that one of my horses had won. Not quite the same as being there, of course. But the satisfaction of putting it all together – of getting the formula right – to make a winner was just as complete. Not bad for a lad whose career in horses began all those years ago at the Western movies.

The lure is still as strong. Maybe the next foal will be the new Northern Dancer that will start a new line of champions. But no matter, because there are so many hidden rewards: to be there when the foal is born, to help it into the world and come out the next morning and see it trotting round the paddock with its mother. And then to watch that little baby grow, develop a little character of its own, its own mannerisms, then get up at dawn to watch it being trained and keep an eye on it whatever it does wherever in the world. The fact is it is part of your family. And that will not change.

CHAPTER 14
Secrets of a Horse Trader

The business of the two-day visit had been done, and the car headed back across the bridge of the Orange River away from the stud farm in the Karoo desert and along the arrow-straight road that stretched over the horizon and beyond to Bloemfontein and the flight home to Johannesburg.

It had been intensive work, involving tours out on the range to see the mares and their new foals; inspecting the young horses in their stables; and looking sadly at a new foal that was so ill it was only a matter of time before the inevitable happened, and wondering why we had used all our expertise to keep it alive in a vain hope that we could change its fate. Then, too, there had been the long and intensive discussions about bloodlines and which stallions should cover which mares in hopes of breeding the best qualities of both. There had been time, too, to find a bag of old golf balls and a rusty seven iron and go down to a dusty paddock in my cowboy boots and hit a few shots. It is as a great violinist once said: 'The public may not notice that I do not practise one day. But I know. And that is what matters.' Not only that, I miss the routine. Even in his late seventies Sir Henry Cotton hit a few shots every day. It was the habit of a lifetime. In my case I like to keep the swing oiled if only with a few shots. Most of them that day had flown as I wished. One of the stable lads had retrieved the golf balls and I took satisfaction that he did not have far to reach between shots.

There had been time for me to rise just after dawn and be alone and sit at the water's edge of the dam at the foot of the mountain and watch the wildlife and gaze across the desert plain. It is the most tranquil place and I thought how much a moment and a place like this would help all those highly-stressed business executives to forget their problems. I take pleasure in the simple things in life and I make no excuse for it. I suppose life itself at times can appear to be quite baffling. I have heard from friends who have visited India of people dying in the streets, and for a moment I cannot but wonder why God allows this to happen. There is no answer. Maybe it is their turn for a wonderful existence in the next life. I do not know. Such thoughts occur in the solitude of Colesberg just after daybreak. I sit by the dam and watch the birds. As a matter of fact I can make most of the bird calls, and sometimes they become so curious they come towards me. I watch an army of ants digging earth from the ground. Eventually they build what must appear to them to be something the size of a stadium. It seemed that everywhere I looked that morning there was an example of purpose and creation.

The previous evening I had dined with my stud manager Ken Twort, a fine gentleman, and his family, and a neighbouring horse breeder and his wife who had called by. She flies her own light plane around the country instead of taking a car; she regaled us with stories of nasty moments in the air and even recalled every detail of the time her father crash-landed in the bush close to the farm he was about to visit. I have to admit that as much as I have flown in my career, I still get nervous in bad weather. I think it stems from a nasty experience my family and I had in a light plane while flying between tournaments in Connecticut some years ago. We flew into a savage storm and suddenly the plane was thrown about violently. A small television set came out of its brackets and items of luggage, cups and food were hurled about. We dropped a very long way and my children were panic-stricken. In truth, so was I. The pilot said it was the worst moment he had ever experienced, even though it did not last long. One of my daughters was so afraid that it was a long time before she stepped into a light aeroplane again. These days, though, she flies all around the world.

At Colesberg, we were about to come to an important decision about whether, after fifteen years, to move the entire stud operation back to Johannesburg on to my farm at Blair Atholl, where more customers could see the horses. I knew that ultimately that decision was mine; but it could wait. There were more pressing matters. We had the horses to consider.

My bloodstock agent John Freeman is a remarkable man with a computer-like knowledge of the history and pedigree of hundreds of horses, and he also possesses a genuine love of the animals. He says that the hairs on the back of his neck still stand up when he sees a horse of rare quality. But then, he has been around horses all his life. Equally importantly, he speaks his mind. He is not afraid to tell people – myself included – what they may not want to hear. We were standing in a paddock looking at the mares and the foals. John and I knew we would have to cut down the number of mares if we moved back to Johannesburg and I wondered whether we should keep just a few more than we had planned. John said: 'Gary, don't go soft on the mares. We ought to sell half the mares. Give me an argument why we shouldn't.' It was boisterous, straight-from-the-shoulder stuff. John knew he had to take a strong line with somebody like myself who sees beauty in every animal. That said, I have to remind myself constantly that all my horses must be for sale. This, to me, is a business. I do not collect them. I trade in them, for profit (I hope) but also for the satisfaction it brings me of getting the formula right.

Now John and I were in the car and homeward bound; but still there was a particular matter to discuss. How should we sell shares in a stallion we were to bring into the country? It can be a precarious business, because this character was coming from the United States and sometimes the transatlantic journey can be unsettling for horses. They suffer from jet-lag and become listless and can lose considerable weight. Moreover if they are given mares within a short time of their arrival, they do not cover them very well. We were well aware of the problems as we prepared to bring over this son of the legendary Northern Dancer and we decided to give him at least six months to acclimatize so that he felt fully at home before we put him to work. We were taking no chances before we showed people what we had to offer. I said: 'I think we have to get hold of the guy in New Zealand and get him to take some pictures of the foals there so we can show people what foals he has.' John had another thought: 'I wonder if I can have copies of a video made. I did that with Jungle Rock. It was just the right idea. Potential customers feel so much closer to the horse.' I warmed to the idea: 'Maybe we should get a professional to go in there and make a proper video. It can't cost much. Maybe a couple of thousand dollars.'

This was the horse business I loved and the aspect of it I rarely had the chance to savour: being present, dressed in khakis and cowboy boots, and getting involved. Only that morning before we left, I noticed one of the trees I had planted had started to wither, even though there was a hosepipe nearby taking water to another part of the farm. I took a knife and cut a hole in the pipe so the ailing tree received a constant spray. Then I told one of the lads to patch up the hose when the tree recovered. It was a small task but one of the essential chores that are part of day-to-day life on a farm. For the rest of my year, my only contact with this existence was likely to be via fax machine in some far-off hotel. Even so, I still feel involved because I am kept informed daily of all that goes on. I could name instantly nearly all the forty mares and not only their sires but also the names of their foals of the previous year.

Wherever I am in the world, I keep myself informed of every aspect of the business, from which of my horses are running to how my shares in the stallions are doing. If my manager says there is an interesting horse coming up for sale then first I ask him to send me a copy of the bloodline. I study it and make a few enquiries, then ask my son Marc, as well as John and manager Ken, to decide the limit to which we should go at the sales. That is another thing. I am aware of all the sales that are going on; aware of the other horses that are winning. In a way it is all very similar to the world of golf, in that you know who is playing well, who is winning, who struggles and who is almost coming back into form.

We have a successful team. When I started, I was not a realist. Every horse looked like a champion because I wanted it to be. But some of them really were dogs. Eventually I learned it was important to pursue only the best bloodlines. Thus the winners began to emerge for us. There have been hundreds, but the Classic champions stand out in my memory. We bred the winner of the South African Derby and of the Natal Guineas. We also bred the winner of the Administrator's Cup in Natal, one of the premier races in South Africa, and we produced a horse called Creator who was the champion two-year-old in the country.

As we drove back to the airport, I reflected on the pictures we had seen of the progeny in New Zealand of this impressive stallion we were about to bring to South Africa.

'John, those foals I saw were so good. I mean so good. And I looked at everyone of those legs. You know, they were so good.'

'Gary, all that worries me is that he had two crops in America . . .'

'. . . Only one in America.'

'Anyway, seven foals in America. Two crops in Australia and two in New Zealand. That means you've got third season syndrome before you've even started.'

As its name implies, this particular condition occurs when the horse has worked constantly for several years and either fails to cover mares adequately or else produces stock of inferior quality. It is always a worrying factor to be considered.

I brightened at another, idea: 'Yes. But it will be first season over here in South Africa.'

'Doesn't matter.'

'On the other hand that is the gamble you take. What happens if they run well?'

'Well, Gary, suddenly you've earned yourself a champion.'

'And so has everybody else, John. That's why the stud fee is so reasonable. We make this very clear to everybody. But what happens if the horse became a superstar? What happens if he became another Northern Guest? Can we say, "Look guys, we have had this tremendous offer to send him back to the States" and do it? Supposing we are offered an abnormal amount of money. Can we do something like that?'

'It's simple, Gary. If there are forty shares, you must make sure you've got twenty-one shares, then the decision to sell is always yours.'

He had already devised a sales strategy with Ken Twort and explained: 'Ken and I will send a letter to the people we want to participate and with the letter will be the video.'

We knew that our reputation precedes us in such deals; prospective buyers know our track record and what they will be getting. With all due modesty, our organization is consistently ranked among the top twenty-five breeders in the country, and sometimes much higher, with such champion horses as Foreign Source and World Over. We have led the way in innovative ideas in horse breeding, including the introduction of the Mare Heat Detector. Originally this device was used on cows and pigs but we adapted it in conjunction with an electrical engineer and the veterinary department of a South African university so that it could be used effectively on horses. Essentially, the machine registers the chemical change in the mare a few hours before ovulation. We had nine problem mares who had gone an entire season without getting into foal. When we got the timing right with this instrument, eight of the mares were subsequently in foal. Also, I put money aside for continuing research into ways we can improve our breeding methods. This very important aspect of the business I learned from leading breeders around the world who made it quite clear that once you are in the business, you have to be aware of every development and new idea otherwise you are left far behind.

I am sure that my reputation as a golfer has opened many doors for me in the horse world and I have been fortunate to speak to the very best breeders, learn from them and pass the information back to my farms in South Africa. I know the team back there realizes that to stay in business we must compete and that, just as in golf, once a high standard has been set, even the slightest fluctuation is regarded as a massive decline by others.

I am not a betting man. If my trainer rings me up to tell me one of my horses is running, I will simply pass the information on to the ladies who work in our house at Blair Atholl so they can have a bit of fun. I like to make life exciting. You have a choice: you can make it exciting or dull. I know which I prefer.

So now the visit was almost over. The car reached the outskirts of Bloemfontein and I was still deep in thought as we drove past Schoeman Park golf course on the way to the airport. There was a professional tournament in progress and my son Wayne was playing, but I would learn how he got on when I spoke to him by phone later. At the airport I took some tea, then sat in the lounge and drew up a list of my friends who might be interested in buying a share of the stallion. Then I smiled as I remembered a phone call I received from a friend of mine in California.

'Gary, where can I buy a 737?'

'Is that a BMW 737?' I asked.

'No . . . a Boeing 737!' He might run to a share!

At the check-in desk the man ahead of me loaded his bag of golf clubs and suitcase on to the scales. He heard a voice say: 'I hope you are hitting them straighter than I am.' He turned round and stared at the khaki shirt and trousers, the cowboy boots and the hat. A smile of recognition spread across his face. He asked for an autograph and I obliged. With that simple gesture I realized Gary Player had stepped back into the world of golf. A public figure once again with all the obligations that imposed. Still, on the aeroplane it was possible to close my eyes and dream of the next visit to my horses – whenever that might be.

CHAPTER 15
The Fruits of Success

Not that it is any of their business, but whenever people ask me how rich I am, they always receive an honest and simple answer. I have no idea. I am not obsessed by wealth, even though I remember what it was like to be poor. Basically I remain the same chap who started off in cheap bed-and-breakfast lodgings on the European Tour, who still searches for his tee-peg and is reluctant to forget a lost golf ball. I leave the high finance to others.

Of course, there is always wild speculation about money, which I find embarrassing and intrusive. Only recently a South African financial magazine concluded that the Gary Player Group – a leisure organization which extends from golf course design and management, travel and real estate development, to brand endorsements – was 'a big business in anyone's book'. When I first started in competitive golf, it never occurred to me that one day I would be making as much impact on the financial pages as in the sports section and that somehow my financial affairs would at times attract as much attention as my golf. I never set out to be rich; never really dreamed of millionaire status. That was never the purpose of all the dedication, hard work and travel, all the relentless physical discipline. I wanted simply to be the best. I was not in it for the money, although I knew that very little could be achieved in my chosen career without a healthy bank account to finance all the expense of travel and hotels and caddies.

The only reason I was able to get married to Vivienne in 1956 was that I won the $14,000 first prize in an Ampol tournament in Australia. I sent her a cable: 'Buy the wedding dress.' We had been absolutely broke at the time and I was investing what money I had in air tickets to tournaments all over the world in the hope of some healthy dividend. Certainly the Australian venture paid off but in those days the only additional source of income to a tournament golfer outside prize money was to be found in endorsements from club and ball contracts and bonuses for successes. True enough, in

Britain many professionals still kept the security of a club job but this was always a compromise which never really worked out. I remember Peter Alliss, who in 1957 was club professional at Parkstone in Dorset, telling me that when he returned to his shop after an incredible three-week stint in which he won the Spanish, Portuguese and Italian Open championships, he was greeted by an irate member who said: 'Alliss, where the hell have you been? I've been waiting for a lesson!'

Not for me. In any case the competition was too stiff to be tackled in anything less than full-time fashion and this also meant there was an added reason to head for the United States Tour where the prize money was large enough to sustain a full-time assault – quite apart from being the area of the world where all the great players were to be found and three of the four major championships were played. So it was that I arrived on the US Tour when the game was on the threshold of its massive boom in popularity; and in the fullness of time I became fascinated by the commercial ideas and philosophies propounded by a young Cleveland lawyer named Mark McCormack who had become Arnold Palmer's manager.

McCormack realized that the earning period of a successful sportsman – certainly at his peak – was fairly short, and it seemed only fair that if everybody else (golf equipment manufacturers, sponsors, etc.) made huge sums out of such success and popularity, then the sportsman himself was entitled to a fair share, which at that time he was not getting. This was not a case of the 'broken-down boxer syndrome' in which everybody takes a piece so there is nothing left for the man who made it all possible. Still, Mark had a valid point and I signed up with him in 1960 before, as he says, the majority of American golf enthusiasts knew who I was. They were soon to find out.

As the game broadened and we – Palmer, Player and, later, Nicklaus – emerged as household names through our success, it became possible to market us to endorse a select range of products all over the world. The simple logic was that it made more economic sense to launch a product using a well-known public hero as part of the sales process than to try to establish a new name coast-to-coast. It was a pioneering era in which all of us were involved in a great adventure: we were being offered income from a variety of sources quite apart from the customary golf-related areas, as the game – and particularly its stars – could be used to sell anything. For this, of course, we paid a commission to our manager, so that he too became a wealthy man. That was the time when Mark, who seemed to get by on a minimum amount of sleep, even found time to meet me at airports and act as my unofficial chauffeur. Moreover, he was personally involved in every negotiated deal on our behalf, the most hilarious of which occurred in 1961 as two club manufacturers attempted to prove which of their products was better for me to use. The argument was whether fibre-glass shafts were better than steel shafts and my signature on a contract depended on it. The steel shaft expert said it was possible to twist the heads off fibreglass shafts and he grabbed one of his rival's samples and did so. At that moment, the fibreglass expert claimed it was possible to bend the steel shaft clubs over his knee and he did so. Then each man began grabbing the other's golf equipment and repeating the process until they were left with two sets of mangled golf clubs. Even so, the fibreglass deal was more attractive, so I played with them and won the 1965 US Open; however, I became increasingly aware subsequently that I could not play consistently with them, and eventually the deal ran its term and we did not renew.

This, then, was the sort of friendly and intimate working relation-ship that existed between Mark and myself and was maintained even when his group of clients was extended not only into other sports, with Jean-Claude Killy, Björn Borg and Jackie Stewart (among others), but also into the realms of entertainment. We were both proud that our agreement had been secured by a handshake, as it had been with Arnold Palmer, and built on an implicit trust that can only come from unquestioning friendship. I must say that no matter how huge and international Mark's organization has become, that bond still exists. In those early days of our relationship, my golf remained the most important thing and I was happy for Mark and his company, the International Management Group, to handle all my business affairs outside South Africa. After all, I did not see myself as a businessman and even to this day when I sit in on board meetings of my own group, I observe one simple rule: 'Trust instinct to the end though you cannot render any reason.' It remains the safest approach to business for me.

Jack Nicklaus, however, was a different kind of person and I suspect he wanted to be at the centre of all his activities – the hub, as it were, at the centre of the wheel of all his operations. He wanted to make all the decisions about his business affairs and by 1970 had departed to form his own Golden Bear International. Another part of his reason may have been that he felt he needed more personal attention and was not happy to remain part of an expanding clientele. I saw no such conflict, because even though Mark McCormack himself became engrossed in wider issues, he assigned a shrewd, able and very personable young Scot, Alastair Johnston, to look after my affairs and that arrangement endured for twenty years. To this day, he is a close friend whose judgement I trust completely.

What I did realize, however, was that new golf heroes were emerging – even though some of them did not stay very long – and they captured public imagination and commercial attention while we sleeping giants of the game, if not eased into the background, were at times moved out of the limelight. In 1980 my son Marc, who had trained with IMG, told me that he felt it was possible for my interests to be developed in a way he felt was commensurate with the name and value of Gary Player. He felt there were more business opportunities to be addressed. Even my farms in South Africa were regarded as simply an expensive hobby. Marc reminded me that I was something of a gentleman farmer because of my other commitments, and that I was being allowed to do my own thing as long as I could afford it and was having fun. But it made sound economic sense that the farming activities should be structured properly as agricultural entities; that some of those activities should be consolidated and made into successful businesses instead of being just bottomless and expensive pits.

Marc had a point. I owned a timber farm in the Cape Province from which we exported to mills around the world. There was my stud farm at Colesberg, also in the Cape. There was another place at Honey Dew with a couple of hundred acres and horses in training. There was a beach home at Plettenberg Bay and another place in Natal. I employed a couple of able business managers in South Africa but their role was simply to keep an eye on things – particularly the running of the farms and purchase of horses while I was away on tour. It was an extremely capital-intensive activity because they had to supervise the budgets and determine how they were apportioned as well as looking for deals, opportunities and licensing offers in South Africa. In short, they looked after the store very competently while I was away but we had no long-term strategy.

Mark McCormack and his team had always regarded South Africa as my home patch. It was my principal residence and all my activities there – horses, farming – were considered 'Gary Player's recreational pursuits' which I would go back to and enjoy almost as rest and recuperation from the onerous demands of world golf. But Marc, my son, sensed that there was more to it than this. He too realized that there was a wider market for a name that had become part of golf lore. As he said: 'You have transcended the need ever to win again. Not to put too fine a point on it, you are already a legend. It is time to earn the rewards.' He was also brutally frank in suggesting that my time on the Seniors Tour would be limited. Perhaps there would be another five years of making impact by winning tournaments. Yet it was vitally important to benefit from associations and relationships that did not depend on that sort of thing any more.

Quite a salesman. I agreed to let him try, just in South Africa at first. That was ten years ago: now he heads a staff of eighty-four specialists. The Gary Player Group of companies has offices in Johannesburg, London, Palm Beach Gardens and Singapore. It is divided into four divisions which handle all my business in various parts of the world, in conjunction with the International Management Group. The farming side of my life stands outside the Gary Player Group and is financially strong enough now that it no longer needs to be funded. It was simply brought into line. We got out of certain activities, sold off various other parts and concentrated on my main love of breeding Thoroughbred racehorses. It is a matter of public record that today my stud farm is ranked among the top twenty in South Africa and that some of our yearlings have fetched the highest prices: sales of horses at times have reached a total of R1 million in a year. As Marc forecast, the breeding business was transformed into a money-maker.

We decided to establish the group of companies when requests for me to design golf courses worldwide began to increase and we realized that more provision needed to be made to cater for all aspects of the work involved. Essentially, there are four companies: Design, Management, Development and Enterprises. We divided our world operation into four quadrants and set up offices to look after all these aspects. Our spheres of operation are the United States, Europe, the East and southern Africa (which takes in surrounding territories including Swaziland, Namibia, Zimbabwe and the islands in the Indian Ocean and even pushes up into Kenya). Since 1980 there have been sixteen golf courses either completed, under construction, in the design stage or under contract in South Africa. Worldwide, there are another forty-seven in various stages of development. When construction begins, each project has a full-time co-ordinator to ensure our designs are followed scrupulously and that the work is carried out as planned. Quite honestly, it is not much good showing a contractor in, say, Thailand a contour map of a golf course if he has never seen one in his life. Left to his own devices he is quite likely to disregard the plan, which is why it is important to have an expert on hand to explain what is needed and then see that it is carried out.

What I bring to each of these projects is my philosophy of golf course design and, equally important, my judgement as to whether the test as designed has the kind of playability when it becomes a reality to make it valid and enjoyable. On each project I am contracted to make certain visits during the two-year construction period but sometimes I find it very difficult to stay away from the site and become more deeply involved. On the Duke of Edinburgh course at Wentworth, for example, I put in a total of fourteen visits because I was so keen to ensure everything went according to the joint plan produced by John Jacobs, Bernard Gallacher and myself.

As an employer, I believe in building incentives into any plan of work so our senior executives are shareholders in the design company and the remainder of the team are offered attractive financial packages and profit incentives that encourage better productivity.

Once the design business was in operation, it occurred to us that after we had completed and handed over a project, we should be offering a complete range of management services to ensure the complex ran efficiently. Thus there was a need for Gary Player Management Services to run the clubs, structure the membership programmes, set up and supervise the maintenance programme and take on the overall management. The attraction for us is not merely the fees we receive for running the various aspects of the club, but that we can also control the product once we have built it to ensure it remains as good as when we handed it over and that members and visitors are happy with it. In this way, too, we also keep in touch with the developer to learn what his next project may be!

The Gary Player Development Company is a natural progression from this operation. We have put together a team that has learned a great deal over the years in building various golf courses. We have worked with most of the major finance houses and banks. We have worked with contractors. We have worked with developers. Historically, we had just been part of the professional team once it has all been put together. We designed for a fee or we managed for a fee. What we realized was that we had the experience and know-how to identify existing pieces of land or property which, in our professional judgement, had exciting potential; so we decided to acquire options and put together our own development package.

It might seem a risk but it turned out to be minimal. I have been very aware of how some of my fellow professionals have lost their money, for a variety of reasons – marriage problems, expensive divorces, bad business deals, bad advice – and I would not entertain any scheme that put all my hard-earned money at risk. The process we followed allayed my fears: one European project is a good example of how it is structured. We discovered a *château* with land on which a golf course had been approved but with which nobody was doing anything. We put a team together. We raised the capital, started work on the course, acquired permission for a hotel and instantly re-capitalized the business by attracting an additional partner. As a result, our initial up-front financial risk was taken care of and we now have a piece of the back-end or 'sweat equity' for having put the deal together. We also take fees from the project in terms of work done by our design company and the management company. And there are also personal fees for me if I am involved in promotional work – company days, personal appearances, exhibition matches and the like.

The scope of developments in golf is enormous and challenging and our plans include a company called Gary Player Resorts in which our project partners put up the money and we source the sites, generally already in existence in recognized resort areas, that can be transformed into highly attractive golf complexes. We have looked at sites in Arizona, California, Florida, Utah and North Carolina; and in Scotland, Portugal and other parts of continental Europe; and the sums involved can reach several million dollars before we even commence our rebuilding and improvement work.

Our biggest assets are the name Gary Player and the group of experts in our companies who know the business. It is an attractive proposition for, say, an investor who on his own would probably be charged three times the proper price for a piece of land on which to build a golf course. But we know the market and that helps the client. For us, of course, there is much more revenue to be earned from this comprehensive service than from simply designing the course. Gary Player Enterprises, in association with IMG, generates the off-course revenue – the commercial affiliations with businesses and resorts, the associations, licensing, merchandising and selling of the name and time of Gary Player. Marc has re-shaped our policy on all of this so that whereas in the past we would sign short-term deals for a flat fee and a royalty of the product being sold, we decided to build long-term joint venture relationships. The Gary Player Golf Equipment Company in South Africa which makes the Anvil, Avenger and Black Knight range of clubs is a good example of this philosophy.

We also seek to own a piece of the joint venture companies that are established in order to develop opportunities all over the world, long after I am a competitive force in the game. In short, we now get involved with partners who have the capital to which we add our knowledge of the golf industry and the impact of the Player name. On the American Seniors Tour there is huge worldwide television exposure for many of our events which helps to keep the name in front of the public. But clearly I have reached that time in my career when it is right to build deals that are not dependent on winning, from which so many one-off deals are struck. Of course, they are still important, in that a tournament win on prime-time television is valuable exposure for the company which has paid a large sum to have its name on a visor or shirt or golf bag. But there now has to be a selective blend of quality and permanence in a product to attract my selling power.

We have also established a Travel and Tours Division which handles a project very close to my heart. There is a range of special safari tours, some of which my brother Ian is involved with, which will take visitors to see a side of Africa normally hidden from view because it is off the beaten track. One of the objectives is to raise funds for the African Wildlife Heritage Trust to combat poaching and the carnage of wild animals. There are art and photographic expeditions which can take in the Okavango Delta, the world's largest natural oasis, the legendary hunters of the Kalahari, or the battle-grounds where Zulu warriors and the British redcoat soldiers fought in 1879 in the battle that shook the British Empire. We have also devised golf-related tours in which I host a small group of enthusiasts to one of the four major championships in world golf, during the course of which we will play a friendly match together. Since I am obliged to travel to these famous venues to compete, it seemed an obvious and attractive development to show a selected few executives around and use my experience.

Gary Player Enterprises also handles the instructional videos and the books, the personal appearances and the challenge matches. In fact, if I consult my diary I already have some definite appointments scheduled a year from now.

That is the problem. There is so little time to answer all the demands that are made on me, particularly while playing golf remains so important in my life. I devote thirty weeks of every year to tournament golf, either the championships or other special events in which I am committed to play. But at the beginning of each of those weeks I am almost certain to be visiting one of my golf course developments to supervise the work. That sort of neat planning is not always possible. I have to spend at least seventy-five days a year on my golf course design work and occasionally it throws up a conflict of interest. I played a tournament in Hawaii and was offered a considerable sum to stay on an extra day to play an exhibition match with Lee Trevino. But I was also asked to spend time on my golf design project in Palm Springs and I knew I needed to fly across the United States to be prepared for the next tournament which began mid-week in Florida. So there was the choice. Earn that sum from a day's work in Hawaii? Or forget about the cash and visit the design project with one of the biggest developers in the world? As a matter of fact, I did both. And then went on and won the tournament.

I am fortunate to have my son Marc involved in my organization because he takes two views of my role. He says: 'You are first and foremost my father. But you are also the boss. I know when you are getting tired. And when you need time off. I will cut and cancel things ruthlessly to give you that time. I know you well enough.' They all thought that when I reached my mid-forties, I would decline competitively on the Regular Tour and give myself more time for golf course design. That might have been the case but along came the Seniors Tour and gave us all a second life. Life has not slowed down; it has got faster.

I have about three weeks away from golf during the year. This is the period when I can stop being Gary Player and enjoy all the other aspects of my life – the home, the children and grandchildren, the horses. I spend two weeks around Christmas and the New Year with all the family when we go down to our beach house, although I cannot spend more than a day lying in the sun with nothing to do. Around that time, too, I like to get down to the stud farm in the Karoo to see the horses and their foals and make plans for the season with my bloodstock agent and stud manager. It is a marvellously remote place and I find time to get away to reflect and to be on my own. The truth is that is takes me very little time to recharge my personal batteries and I find it refreshing, for example, just to go out and plant trees – even in the lashing rain – on my farm at Blair Atholl. That closeness to nature is all I need to lift me up.

My family says I am like a chameleon. When I talk to a gardener I am a gardener myself; I become a stable lad when around horses; and so it goes on. I suppose part of it is the escape from the obligations of being the person the world knows as Gary Player. My staff and my family know that I do not like arguments or rows. Of course I get angry and upset at times but I think all of them know the moment I become serious, and at business meetings my executives know my life is compartmentalized and they have only a specific part of it. If the meeting drags on unnecessarily, they know I will get up and go, saying: 'That's it, fellows. I am out of here.' They also know I will not touch an endorsement, no matter how much money is offered, if I disapprove of the product, so there is no point in even mentioning the idea to me. Two cigarette companies offered huge sums but I turned them down; nor will I endorse any alcoholic drinks.

So how do I enjoy the fruits of all this success? Well, I am not obsessive about material possessions. And when I am travelling one hotel is very much like another so there is little opportunity to feel like a rich man even if I wished. In fact the money generated by the group is reinvested into fixed assets, land for example, in various parts of the world.

It is all a long way from those early days when I used to wash my sports shirt in the bedroom basin between rounds and I was ticked off by Humphrey McMasters, then boss of the Slazenger company, for dragging my golf bag along the pavement: 'Gary, my dear fellow, what are you doing to our equipment? You are rubbing out the name of Slazenger!'

They tell me I could retire tomorrow, fly around the world to see the classic Thoroughbred horse races, meet my old friends and just play a little golf. That thought frightens me. Maybe that is why I simply want to remain Gary Player the Golfer and let others I trust look after Gary Player the Businessman.

CHAPTER 16
The Evolution of a Golf Swing

My golf swing in its original form can best be summed up in some advice a senior professional gave me when I first arrived in Britain more than thirty-five years ago. He took one look and suggested I go home and find myself a safe, well-paid club job. There was no future for me, he said, in tournament golf.

That was more than 157 tournament wins, including nine major titles, ago. He was right, of course, about a job as a club professional being safe and well-paid. He follows that kind of lucrative vocation these days. But in truth he had a point. Even professionals back in South Africa had warned me – more cruelly – that with a swing like mine all I would ever do was eat beans. Clearly they did not see it as being consistent enough for me to make a living from producing good scores. In fact, when I came to Britain the distinguished and perceptive golf writer Pat Ward-Thomas reflected: 'His swing is abnormally flat, the face of the club is shut at the top and his grip, with the right hand well over the shaft, most unorthodox ... but Player was successful with it because he was a natural games player.' But even the technique that Mr Ward-Thomas observed was a great improvement on that with which I started my career as a professional golfer. In simple terms, because of my stature, I was always obliged to launch myself fiercely at the ball so that it seemed that I was giving close to one hundred per cent effort and power whenever I made contact. Even my initial four-knuckle grip with the left hand was an admission of the need to gain precious distance from the hooking right-to-left trajectory that grip imparts on the ball to give it extra impetus. That was, of course, on the good days. For much of the time I was quite erratic; but somehow even in those early days, I managed to keep a score together. I had what is known as the ability to fight for a score.

My boss Jock Verwey, the professional at the Virginia Park club in Johannesburg who later became my father-in-law, warned me that I had to change my grip and alter the upright plane of my backswing if

I really wanted to make significant progress in the game. I ignored his advice for a year, even though I suspected he was substantially correct. The plain fact of the matter is that at the very peak of competitive play it is essential to have total reliability of technique; or rather, it is impossible to beat opponents if at the same time you are trying to combat and contain intrinsic flaws and weaknesses in your own swing. As I have emphasized before, in extreme moments of pressure, when the adrenalin flows, the excitement is at fever pitch and the concentration is almost at a dream level, there is time only to aim and fire. To be obliged in such moments to guard against a tendency to hook is a ruinous distraction. And yet in those days on my first visit to Britain, John Jacobs, the highly respected golf teacher and now my close friend and co-designer of the new Wentworth Edinburgh course, observed that although my swing was flat and very much round the body, it was consistent; and curiously enough the ball always landed softly, even with the hooking trajectory.

So how had this ugly-looking swing that seemed to have no future come into existence? Why I had I not burst upon the world with a flawless copybook technique? The reason was simple enough. I learned golf in a strange way. For much of the time I learned to play without using a golf ball. More precisely, I drilled my swing without coming into contact with a ball. As a schoolboy I could get to the golf course only at the weekends, so for the rest of the time I would complete my homework every evening then practise and practise my golf swing on a black rubber mat in our garden – never knowing where the imaginary ball might have gone. Thus the technique was fashioned, and it remains an inescapable fact that the basic form and outline of your original technique rarely changes, no matter how many adjustments and refinements are made. For that reason of course, it is always possible to recognize a golfer by his action even from a considerable distance away.

One thing that became obvious to me about the hitting action was that the weight had to be transferred from the back foot to the leading foot to build up momentum in order to deliver any kind of proper force and striking power. It is a principle that holds true in tennis, as well as in boxing where the weight has to be transferred before a substantial blow can be thrown. These days it is part of my teaching routine – and not a bad personal check – to stand on a pair of bathroom scales and just determine how the weight is distributed at the address position, the top of the backswing and the follow-through. When similar tests were carried out on Greg Norman, it was discovered that 90 per cent of his weight was in his left side after he had struck the ball – which among other considerations goes a long way to explaining his big-hitting prowess. It is clearly one of the intrinsic problems of a golf swing which starts from a static position that a way must be found to generate the momentum with the necessary body movement to cause this weight shift, while operating within geometrically defined limits.

Even in those early days, observers detected what they considered to be the secret of my technique; or rather, the reason I could make this ungainly swing function efficiently. I possessed a suppleness of body action – a flexibility of muscle – that allowed me to coil my body to an extreme degree in order to generate the power needed to keep up with the longer hitters, although, as a result of that boyhood accident when I broke my neck, I still did not have as much neck freedom as I would have liked. This suppleness also allowed me to produce a big movement of the left hip from the top of the backswing which ensured not only that the weight was transferred for the strike but also that my body was, as it were, 'out of the way' of the hitting area so that arms, hands and club could arrive on target with maximum force.

I had, of course, watched all the great players at work on the practice ground. I had tried their methods and when they failed I reverted to my old style. When I went to the United States in the late 1950s I had the chance of playing with the legendary Ben Hogan in several tournaments. He had been my idol since boyhood. More than this, he was a role model. He epitomized a dedication to the game that inspired me and made me want to follow his example. He was not satisfied with anything less than the highest standards from himself. The stories about his dedication became legendary: how he would hit a succession of full wood shots one-handed without having to re-grip the club; how he detected a flaw in his fairway wood shots when he became fatigued and deliberately tired himself out on the practice ground so that he could study himself in this state. This truly was the stuff of heroes and I absorbed every scrap of information about the man. His total obsession with the pursuit of the ultimate golf technique made him appear to be an aloof, rather grey figure. And true enough, he was a man of few words with a very brusque manner. When he was non-playing captain of the 1967 American Ryder Cup team at the Champions Club in Houston, he looked quite disdainful when Arnold Palmer asked him in the locker-room before a practice round: 'Ben, have you got any of those small British golf balls that we could use?' In those days the size of golf ball was optional, but obviously the smaller 1.62in diameter British ball flew farther than the larger American 1.68in size, although it was not so easy to control in the short game and on the putting green. To Hogan it was inconceivable that Arnold had obviously not had the foresight to practise with the small ball before he arrived for the match. Ben gave him a withering look and growled rather sarcastically: 'Did you remember to bring your clubs? Anyway, who says you are playing?'

For a time Ben and I seemed to hit it off rather well, as though both aware of each other's pursuit of perfection and absolute dedication to it. It was even said that he advised me to 'weaken' my grip by placing the left-hand thumb on top of the shaft instead of down the right-hand side. Hogan did not think my swing was unduly flat, but rather that it resembled very much his own swing plane which pleased me because we were of similar stature (around 5ft 9in). He felt that it was my hand position at the top of the backswing which gave the impression of a flat swing, but that it was fine by him.

It is true to say that I learned more by watching Ben Hogan than I ever did by asking for advice from him. In fact, the one time I phoned him and asked for a piece of advice, he said: 'Who do you work for?'

I said: 'Dunlop.'

He replied: 'Well, ask Mr Dunlop.' End of conversation.

None of which detracts from my admiration for him as a golfer and an exponent of technique. Moreover, he paid me a generous tribute in the late fifties when he told an American journalist: 'I know how hard he has worked. He's doing what I've been advocating for a long time. Working hard on fundamentals and then working those fundamentals into his game.'

The Player swing was undergoing change. I had come to terms with my strong grip because I knew I had to minimize the perils of the hook. Hogan had called it 'working on the fundamentals', and the basic truth is that a sound golf swing has to be built on a proper grip. There has not been a great and enduring golfer yet born who did not have an orthodox grip – or at least one that was not so exaggerated as to show too many knuckles on the left hand. It took time and perserverance, but it was achieved; and yet somehow the 'weaker' grip placed even more emphasis on my ability to coil myself tight enough on the backswing to release the essential power at the ball. I developed a wide arc to my backswing with a full extension of my left arm and a complete shoulder turn without too much hip turn. It allowed me to twist the body tight and retain the tension until the

Early days on the US tour with Deane Beman, who quit as a full-time tournament professional to become tour commissioner — the most influential figure in US professional golf.

My parents — Muriel and Harry. Their happiness together was short-lived. My mother died before I became a champion but Harry lived long enough to see that day — and many more!

In spite of his lung complaint (the sad legacy of a lifetime spent down the mines) Harry still insisted on watching me play whenever possible. There was a great bond between us.

A rare chance for Vivienne and I to relax with our first two children, Jennifer and Marc, away from the pressures of my globe-trotting career which was to separate us so often.

Another rare moment. The complete Player family today, at home in Blair Atholl for our 'indaba', the customary annual get-together to discuss family matters. From the left are myself, Theresa, Michelle, Jennifer, Vivienne, Marc, Amanda (seated) and Wayne.

In the 1950s my youthful suppleness enabled me to make a large shoulder-turn in the backswing to release maximum power at the ball.

By the 1990s the swing had evolved into a more open-and-shut hand action to ease strain on my physique.

The 'Big Three' — Arnold, Jack and myself in the glory days of the 1960s when we dominated the major championships.

Thirty years on our friendship still endures, although we continue to be rivals on the field of play. I retain a genuine love and respect for both of them.

The box office appeal of two members of the 'Big Three' — or the day 'Arnie's Army' met 'Player's Pack' at Augusta to cheer their heroes to success. All good natured, although Jack Nicklaus had to overcome some hostility from fans when he challenged Arnold.

Success at the 1968 British Open at Carnoustie. Jack had just been beaten but he was the first to congratulate me — and he really meant it! His turn would come many times and he knew it.

Business – and a banana – as usual despite an armed guard to protect me from the threats of anti-apartheid demonstrators when I competed on the US tour. I refused to give in and run away.

The family that jogs together . . . Vivienne has always shared my love of fitness. She is a top-class swimmer and reached the fringes of international class as a golfer.

Bob Hope, one of the great enthusiasts and benefactors of the game, who promotes his own tournament. When someone asked him if he played much, he cracked 'Just days'.

The King meets the Black Knight. Elvis never quite mastered the royal and ancient game, despite my advice and tuition.

Spare time at home is still rare and precious, even for a grandfather. Lancer, my Alsatian, is always pleased to romp with his master.

Roberto, Jennifer's son, is still happy to kiss his old granddad.

Since boyhood I have loved to be around horses. They are my passion — and as a thoroughbred breeder they take up much of my time. My dream is to produce more champions.

The life of a golf champion is not always confined to the fairways. The 'Big Three' turned golf into big business in the 1960s, which meant that we had to be at home in the boardroom too.

By the 1980s I had established a personal office with staff at my home, quite apart from the headquarters in Johannesburg, London, Palm Beach and Singapore.

The friendship of Willy Betha, my farm foreman, was to become one of the great influences in my life.

Christmas day at Blair Atholl, when all the farm workers and their families come to our house and my family — including grandchildren Roberto and Antonia — are ready to greet them.

A fishing trip with one of my closest friends, Fardell Allem, along the Zululand coast. I am not a keen hunter and prefer to catch my quota on camera!

very last moment before impact in the downswing. If there was a flaw, according to observers, then it was an occasional failure to clear the left hip during the downswing so that the ball was either blocked to the right or, more often than not when this occurred, hooked to the left.

I knew, however, that the character and commitment of my type of swing required maximum flexibility and co-ordination of the body at all times and for a diminutive man this meant I had to be in peak physical shape. Thus my exercise routine took on added importance. When this essential co-ordination was fractionally out of synchroniz-ation the hook could reappear, with devastating effect. A typical example was during my traumatic 1973 season after I had been forced to take three months away from golf following major surgery and could not get all the working parts of my swing functioning in precise order. And while it might have seemed, according to newspaper reports, that I constantly found new cures for the hook with extra-ordinary regularity, the real truth of the matter was that whatever the apparently new suggestion, its simple merit was to help me get my body moving again as it should.

Not quite a gimmick; but not far from it. The golf swing is essentially a question of feel – in other words, how the player perceives it through his muscles – and these little tricks are in every-day use with any golfer who has ever swung a club, no matter what his or her standard may be. For what other reason are those endless volumes of 'How to Play' books produced – my own included – but to pass on these insights and secrets? Even the top players in the world begin to make mistakes in their technique without noticing what they are doing wrong. They see the result of the error, of course, but tracing the fault is another matter.

It is a curious and heartening aspect of this game that rivals will help rivals to seek cures, even if it means they themselves might be beaten when the ailing player is restored to top form. Perhaps this spirit of generosity exists in others sports too, but in golf it can also extend to handing over clubs – drivers, putters, wedges – on per-manent loan if they can help a fellow professional improve his game.

Over the years of competitive play and the necessary constant daily practice needed to keep at peak form, I realized that this immensely strenuous technique would have a limited life, despite my superior fitness which helped it work so well. I learned that a person's mus-cular structure begins to decline from the age of thirty onwards and as the modern golf swing – at least for the younger professionals – is very much a big muscle technique, the period of success with this method could be very short. It employs the strongest and biggest muscles in the body – in the back, thighs, legs, etc. – to generate the momentum to deliver arms, hands and club at the ball forcefully and accurately. It is achieved by coiling the upper body on the backswing against the resistance of the lower body before being unleashed. It does not, therefore, take much medical knowledge to realize that this kind of tension must have residual effects; that lower back trouble can become an occupational hazard; and that the muscles become subject to constant wear and tear, particularly through day-to-day tournament play in which it is clearly not possible to ease off – play, say, at 50 per cent – and still prevail.

I have always felt that I hit the ball hard all the time. I believe that most successful professionals on tour hit it as hard as they can while still keeping it in play. That is why they are so good; and curiously enough, the 'swing track' followed with a full-power swing probably helps to maintain this accuracy because it eliminates any temptation to steer the ball with a softer action. There were, however, times when my technique went off-track despite hitting hard and I could not pick up on my own flaws. I remember after one bad spell, Jock Verwey noticed instantly what was wrong. I had been coming off the ball in my attempt to hit it hard and moving away as I hit it. He just reminded me that my customary action was a 'down and through' move and that thought alone put me back on track.

I was practising for the World Matchplay at Wentworth once when a traffic policeman spotted a slight mistake in my swing. I happily took his advice. I am never too proud to take a tip from anyone if it helps me to play well. As the great Scottish poet Robert Burns wrote:

> O wad some Pow'r the giftie gie us
> To see oursels as others see us!
> It wad frae mony a blunder free us,
> And foolish notion.

Whatever the wider wisdom of those words, they certainly sum up the right approach to curing golf faults. During the 1971 Dunlop Masters at St Pierre in Chepstow, the late Sir Henry Cotton offered me a tip to cure my hooking problems. He suggested that I keep the left heel raised off the ground throughout the swing – or at least until after impact – to ensure that my right hand worked harder to hit the ball. Henry was an avid disciple of the doctrine of strong hands in the golf swing and believed that the raised left heel was a good method of correction for faults when the hands were not working effectively. It was not a replacement method, just discipline to realign the body and make the working parts function in proper sequence. I used the raised-heel method throughout the last round of that tournament and scored 66, and I used it again a week later during the World Match-play championship at Wentworth when I beat Jack Nicklaus in the final.

What became clear to me as I approached the age of forty was that it was time to amend my swing to a more manageable, less onerous movement if I wanted to survive longer in the game. The point, of course, was that my short game, bunker play and putting remained very much undiminished because this was simply a matter of feel that could be sustained by constant and diligent practice. I had, however, experimented with various putting techniques, switching from my customary tapping method, acquired in my boyhood days to over-come the vagaries of bumpy greens, to a more gentle stroke, and then back again to the old method. And by and large the results had remained unchanged. But it was the process by which I manoeuvred the ball within close range of the green that was under review, for it was quite clear that even my high state of suppleness would not be able to sustain the essential reverse C-shape of the body that the golfer achieves after impact, with the head staying back while the rest of the body has moved through as the ball is struck. This kind of swing demands flexibility as well as a strong body and hands and there came a point when I realized I would not be strong enough to make this movement any longer. I had to look round for another method because my desire and ambition were still strong and my short game absolutely solid enough for more victories.

I realized, too, that the enduring champions had all employed a method of swinging that imposed minimum stress on their backs. Instead of keeping the arms and hands passive in the backswing so that the clubface was closed – facing upwards to the sky – at the top, thereby making the success of the strike depend on the degree of body movement, they were altogether more relaxed. Their process was much simpler. They achieved it by 'opening' the clubface – almost rolling the hands to the right – early in the backswing and 'shutting' it – rolling the wrists back towards the left – in the down-swing. The great modern exponent was Irishman Christy O'Connor senior, whose method eventually helped me to overcome my hook tendency. There were others who used the method, including Sam

Snead and Henry Cotton, both great examples of competitive longevity. It meant there was no strain in the backswing, and it was clear
that none of the old champions – Taylor, Braid, Hagen, Sarazen –
ever finished their swings in that reverse C position, yet this had not
affected their scoring skills. If anything, they moved forward, some
of them to such an extent that they were actually walking after the
ball as soon as they had struck it. This clearly proved they had made a
correct weight transference in the hitting zone, which is always the
sign of a well-executed stroke. I experimented with the method and
discovered that as I tried to hit the ball hard, the momentum was such
that I too found myself walking through after the ball, almost as
though I had lost my balance. Indeed, a lot of people who saw me
were convinced I had played a bad shot and pushed the ball to the
right of target, when in actual fact it was perfectly on line. I had found
a way of hitting the ball as hard as before, of maintaining the distance
I required to keep going in championship golf; and all of this had
been achieved without putting additional strain on a physique that
was beginning to need more care.

What can be said is that previously I employed a technique that
only the strongest and the ablest golfers could use successfully; but
this alternative method is one that anybody can use effectively. I also
believe now that it could be used to greater effect by younger professionals who might last longer at the top if the effort of the golf swing
were not quite so onerous.

It is, of course, a significant comment on the modern golf swing –
and, moreover, the general fitness of the top players on tour – that
they are now accompanied by a gymnasium plus qualified staff to
every event. A high proportion of these professionals need daily
exercise and treatment before they can even swing a club on the
practice range. If modern swing techniques develop without due
consideration to the physical side-effects, then the career span of
top-class players could become even shorter. What is needed is
common sense and acknowledgement of values and methods that will
allow them to endure for as long as a man like Sam Snead remained at
the top of his profession.

In modern times the efforts of older fellows – those on the other
side of forty such as Ray Floyd, Hale Irwin, Jack Nicklaus and
myself – underline the importance of an enduring method because it
highlights a unique aspect of this physical sport: that it is not necessarily a young man's game and that good scores do not cease after a
man passes the age of fifty. There is, however, a state of mind to be

considered. A man who feels old really is old. I was forty-two and virtually written off in terms of championship golf when I played in the last round of the 1978 US Masters at Augusta. Even though I was putting together an incredible last round, I sensed there was no interest from the crowd. I suddenly turned to my young playing partner Seve Ballesteros and said: 'Seve, I will tell you something. These people don't think I can win. You watch. I'll show them.' Seve reflected afterwards that he felt I needed this feeling of having to make a point – or believing that people were against me – to bring out the best of my competitive powers. He seemed to feel he could identify with that spirit. My only comment would be that it was not so much the crowd's indifference to which I reacted but rather the reason for that attitude, which I took to be a view that I was past it and no longer a relevant figure. That really did make me respond.

When I won, I punched the air, not in defiance but to express the end of the conquest; and I suppose it is fair to say that I do see competitive golf as much as a battle of wills as a cold examination of skills. The Player punch has become a trademark and is now standard practice by almost everyone in the game – not just at the moment of victory but even when a crucial putt drops. I cannot remember when I first made the gesture. But I know that having worked hard and dedicated myself to the process of winning, it became a natural expression of how I felt when those putts went down and the title was mine.

I feel now as though I could go on playing competitive golf for another ten years with the method I have now perfected. However, I am cautious about making predictions. In the days when I travelled as part of the Big Three, Arnold Palmer said he would never quit. Jack Nicklaus and myself said we would be out of the game by the time we were thirty-five. We are now, of course, both over fifty and each year when we enter the champions' room in the Augusta clubhouse for the US Masters, Arnold is waiting for us. And he smiles.

'Hey, are you two still around? I thought you were gonna quit years ago!' Point taken, Arnie. The game is too good to give up now that an entirely new career has opened up at senior level. My ambition now is to match or even pass Jack's collection of twenty major titles – only I will include the greater span by including Seniors Tour majors as well as those on the Regular Tour. Jack is clearly ahead on the regular tour but I am not sure he will play with the intensity to collect the majors on the Seniors Tour. Desire may have something to do with it. Moreover, he has many commitments elsewhere. But I also suspect that his physique cannot endure the kind of strain his particular technique puts on it. And he may not be prepared to consider any new ideas. But one of my essential philosophies is simply: change is the price of survival. I have seen the truth of this in the number of successful players who are now playing well on the Seniors Tour as they turn fifty and some even approach their sixties. What spurs them is the thought that they can still play, still find self-esteem and a new lease of life. And if, before I am finished, it takes yet another change of method to keep on playing, I will pay that price. Somebody once said I just like winning. That is probably very close to the truth.

CHAPTER 17
The Secrets of a Great Golf Course

An intriguing battle of wits invariably develops between me and anybody who plays a golf course I have created. In a way, it is a personal matter, even though we may never have met. I challenge skill and courage. The golfer finds a way to outfox me. It is a friendly rivalry that will endure for generations to come.

For me, this is the exhilarating aspect of golf course design. All the experience of my professional years, all the great courses I have played worldwide and the principles I have observed upon them have been distilled into what I think a great test should be. It means that for as long as the test exists, thousands of players will be able to set themselves against the values and standards that a certain Gary Player, champion golfer in the second half of the twentieth century, held to be important.

I am also well aware that as the years progress, my own achievements may slide into the dusty corners of the record-book and that people may forget my era of success just as modern-day enthusiasts might scratch their heads about the exploits of Walter Hagen or Harry Vardon. The golf course, however, cannot be ignored. So long as it is played, its creator is remembered, if not by name then by style. It is not a monument but in my case I regard it as testimony to what I believe to be the essential challenge of the game.

There was a famous British architect who once suggested that the ideal golf course should be surrounded by rugged terrain and slopes but the playing area should be flat. I take this to mean that a golf stroke which overcomes fear and intimidation and is properly played should be adequately rewarded. I have tried to follow this philosophy in the golf courses I have designed around the world, because it captures completely the essential challenge of a game that must always seem to be within reach of both the hacker and the good player. But it means the architect must always remember that he is trying to entertain the golfer and not overwhelm him; and perhaps even more importantly, that he is not building a golf course primarily to increase his own reputation. Some modern architects seem to be missing that point – or ignoring it. They are building golf courses on which people cannot even come close to playing to their handicaps. They are building greens so undulating that even the professional cannot handle them and bunkers so deep that the average golfer cannot get out of them. I consider myself a pretty good bunker player but even I was defeated by a sand-trap 10 feet deep I discovered on the PGA West Course in California. I hit ten recovery shots and never got one of them out. There is no logic in that kind of problem.

Some modern architects make other fundamental mistakes as well. They continually put water hazards in front of greens – to which average golfers are taking long irons anyway – or if there is no water they will use a line of bunkers to create unfair problems. What they have done is to remove the flexibility of strategy and playing style from the game. They have imposed only one kind of shot for everybody to hit to a green yet the great charm of this game is that there are many types of shots that can be employed to reach a green. That precept is as old as golf itself and derives from the game in its original form over the sandhills and dunes of the Scottish shores, so that the shots that were played centuries ago are still appropriate today. You can play a lofted shot into the green or a bounce-up shot. A hacker can play it. A champion can play it. And both are tested to their limits.

What I do with my greens is to shape them so that they have a narrow neck where the flag is placed. It means the hacker has the chance to run the ball on to the large part of the green but the good player needs greater skill and judgement if he wants to hit an eight iron or a wedge into the neck and nearer to the flag.

That said, there must be obvious reward for hitting the ball close and I think that if a player strikes, say, a five iron approach some 12 feet from the hole then he or she deserves a perfectly flat straight-in putt or at least one with very little break. For that reason I am in favour of building gentle plateaux into greens so that the player who takes the safe route and hits the ball a long way from the hole must negotiate these undulations when he putts. But my point remains that the hacker must also be given a reasonable chance of at least hitting a green because it doesn't happen very often. If the average golfer puts the ball on the green in regulation figures six times in a round, it's been a great day.

It is fairly easy to recognize a poor golf course: there are certain tell-tale signs which give it away. The most obvious mistake is to build bunkers in the middle of fairways. These traps should always be pushed to the margins of the fairways on either side. The fairway is the landing zone. It is the place at which to aim and a player should not be penalized for achieving that task. The wayward shot – left or right – must be punished by traps and rough but there is a basic injustice in penalizing the stroke that is perfectly aimed and struck.

As much as I adore links golf, I think the bunkering in Scotland is a bit too extreme. Not only are they littered around the fairways but they are deep, which makes it difficult to escape more than 5 yards from them. The best that can ever be done is simply to get the ball out. They therefore eliminate any sort of gamble, which is a vital ingredient of this game. I like knowing that if I gamble and hit a great shot I can get on the green but if I mis-hit the ball, I will stay in the trap and face even more trouble. The element of gamble must never be taken out of golf because it is the one aspect that gives some shots

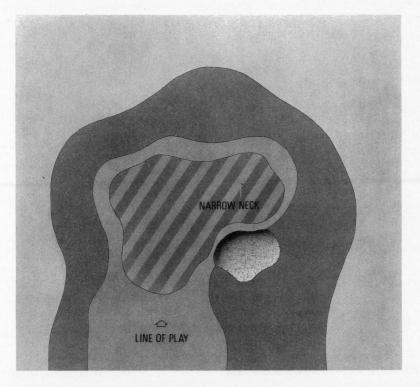

I ensure that a good green gives players of all standards a choice to score. The moderate player can hit to the front edge but faces a long putt. The good player must hit over the bunker to land on the narrow neck of green if he wants a birdie chance.

their importance and lifts the game from a mere test of technique to an examination of courage and self-belief. Let me give an example. The thirteenth hole at Augusta was the best par-five I ever played in my life (until Jack Nicklaus redesigned its green and in my opinion reduced the challenge to a pedestrian exercise), where once titles had been won and lost. In its original form this left-hand dog-leg, which forms part of the notorious Amen Corner stretch of crucial home-ward holes, was the ultimate test. The perfect tee shot took the curve of the fairway but still left a daunting shot to the green over the deep creek which guarded the front edge.

Make a mess of the tee shot, either by being too careful and straying into the trees on the right or by being too bold and bouncing towards the ditch on the left, and the green was out of reach – except in three shots.

But there was always the gamble. Hit a good second shot and the prize was a birdie or even an eagle. Hit a bad one and the punishment could be a six or seven (and possibly the loss of the title, as Curtis Strange discovered in 1985 when he virtually threw away his chances on this hole with a four wood approach that never quite made it and trickled back to the water's edge). It was therefore a magnificent par-five. But Jack undermined its challenge, perhaps unwittingly, by removing the risk element, because he toughened the test to such a degree that it was not worth taking a gamble. In times past, the long second shot always had to favour the left-hand side of the green to avoid the deep creek which ran in front and flanked its right side. But Jack built such fierce undulation and slope into the left of the green that any long approach missing the target gave the player an intimidating recovery. From the left side, it is virtually impossible to chip the ball within 10 feet of the flag. Therefore the long shot was no longer worth the risk. Jack had eliminated at least 30 per cent of the shots that in times past would have gone for the green from the fairway. Instead, these players laid up and played it safe. There is no prize any more for simply getting over the creek. Jack also took away the excitement for the galleries, who loved watching players shoot at the par-five with all the trouble around it. The ideal par-five should be shortish – maybe a driver and a four wood – but with immense trouble around it. It entices you to gamble, rather like a big mouse-trap with a piece of cheese in it. If you can nibble the cheese without the spring going off, you've got it. But make a mistake and you are caught in the trap.

That, in many ways, is the challenge of Augusta. The task at first looks fairly simple. You stand on the tee and gaze at those wide fairways and think you will kill it. But it is not that easy. In a clever way, Augusta allows you to create your own problems. The trouble is obvious and avoidable. It is the element of risk – and the bad shot – that makes people come to grief. The secret of Augusta is the narrowness – from front to back – of its greens. They are wide enough but have very little depth, which means they demand absolute precision, even with the short irons. In these terms, the short twelfth is perhaps the perfect par-three. It measures 155 yards and requires no more than an eight iron or a seven iron, and yet it has ruined many winning chances because the green is virtually a narrow strip between bunkers at the rear and water in front. After all, anyone can create a difficult par-three by making it excessively long. But it takes skill and imagination to produce such a formidable test as this one with more modest dimensions. Its true accolade is that it is the sort of hole you worry about before you even get there. It is a fearsome challenge, not simply because of its sequence in the round at Amen Corner. Even if it were the second hole, it would still hold the same terror. A bad shot would almost certainly mean a double-bogey, and no matter how many holes there are left to play, the golfer would face a formidable task retrieving those strokes while trying not to drop any more.

At Augusta there are at least seven greens that are wider than they are deep and therefore demand this kind of pinpoint precision play. The long downhill second hole requires a tremendous approach shot to reach the putting surface. But the equation is perfect. If it comes off, the rewards are enormous – as Seve Ballesteros found when he eagled the hole to launch a blistering charge towards his first Masters title.

The great charm of golf is that it is played over various terrains and therefore the pitch, as it were, never stays the same. I am convinced, though, that the principles of good design remain unchanged. It is, for example a mistake to design all the par-threes in the same direction because there must always be variation of shot-making in the prevailing wind. Then again, it is a great error to design a lot of uphill holes because they are rarely enjoyable to play and tend to demoralize the higher handicapper. Moreover, they also contravene a fundamental principle of golf course design as far as I am concerned in that one should always be able to see the entire test from the tee (apart, obviously, from the occasional dog-leg; but even then the contour of the ground must yield some clue). For that reason I prefer elevated tees. Not only do they flatter the hacker, because from that height even a bad shot looks good – what the late Sir Henry Cotton called 'the incomparable thrill of driving downhill' – but they also give a fair idea of the layout and terrain to be played. The essential requirement is that the golfer should be able to see where the ball has to be hit.

It can be argued, however, that this is essentially a professional golfer's point of view and that a fundamental challenge for the modern player is to prove his ability to drive 'blind' – in other words, to hit over the hills to an out-of-sight fairway guided only by a marker post. That is still the case on some holes at Royal Troon and it is also probably the major reason why Royal Birkdale has not yet become one of the great golf courses of the world. This magnificent Lancashire course has been the venue for some memorable Open championships and Ryder Cup matches but it possesses what I call the 'hidden flaw': there are about six holes on which the player has to struggle to see the definition of the fairways. If the tees were built perhaps 4 feet higher, Royal Birkdale would be a classic golf course. The purists will argue that such alterations eliminate the traditional importance of local knowledge or the need for a player to do any homework; yet I insist that the quality of shot is not diminished in any way by being able to see the target. Consider the drive that has to be hit from the ninth tee uphill to the spine of a ridge from which the land falls away on either side. It is a completely blind shot and yet it dictates the entire playing strategy of the hole. This is hit-and-hope stuff. More to the point, it reduces everybody to the same mundane task – of simply hitting a fairway that cannot be seen.

These are weaknesses in what I consider otherwise to be a course of great character. What I also look for in a great course is balance in the variety of its eighteen holes, which by the final green should have tested a player's shot-making skills and ingenuity to the full. There must be a proper blend of holes: a par-five that can be reached in two good shots balanced by one that cannot; a long par-four and a shortish one; some short, medium and long par-threes, although I dislike par-threes which measure more than 180 yards. I like to build at least one short hole, around 120 yards, with a tiny green. To build a hole like that, that can make a guy choke when he comes to it, is a real achievement.

What a golf course also needs is what I call elasticity, not simply in terms of being stretched to accommodate the long-hitters but in displaying a variety of tees with bunkers designed to challenge them.

Thus a golf course must be all things to all men. It must be flexible enough to provide a varying challenge for the old lady golfer, the young player and the top professional. That is the skill of golf course design.

For example, in 1979 I was given the specific task of building one of the toughest golf courses in the world as the venue for the Million Dollar Challenge at Sun City: it was intended to test the greatest players in the game for what was the biggest first prize. At the same time, I also designed alternative tees to accommodate all the holiday visitors to the Bophuthatswana resort. The irony of it all was that the tourists still insisted on playing from the back tees and when they could not break 90 they grumbled that it was too tough. But the fact is the course was never designed for them to play that way, even though I had made it possible to reduce it to the sort of size and length they would play at home.

Of course, in general terms, the great virtue of a golf course, wherever it is laid out, is that by and large it observes the character of the landscape – where one exists, of course – and guarantees its survival in unspoilt form. It is also more than likely to preserve the wider environment, even though in certain parts of the world – particularly in Britain – the greenkeeper is in constant conflict with some of the wildlife (rabbits, badgers etc.). The rules of the game even recognize the effect these burrowing animals can have on the sport and make special provision for relief from their handiwork.

There are times, however, say in the Arizona desert or parts of the Californian desert, where the golf designer has to create his own landscape by moving millions of tons of earth by machinery to make mounds and hills from what was originally just a piece of unpromising flat earth. In Alaqua, Orlando, we had to build a golf course out of a swamp. In Palm Springs we went into the desert and built bigger hills and valleys than you would find among the sentinel sand dunes of Royal Birkdale. In principle, though, it is better to build a test that is as consonant with the area as possible. It is equally important to ensure that the right types of shrubs and flowers and foliage are planted so that what is left remains a thing of beauty as well as a superior test of golf. Thus, there is a constant balance to be struck between scenic beauty and the test of skills.

At Alaqua we knew we needed definition of the terrain so we built our tees to a height of 55 feet and used the grass that was typical of that part of Florida in such a way that people do not regard it as being a flat golf course, even though it arose, as it were, from the marshlands. In fact, we have taken advantage of the swamps and wetlands and extended them, and in so doing increased the fish life and the bird life, which has pleased the environmentalists – and, I am sure, the wildlife. In Palm Springs we have built high dunes from the desert floor so that the course plays very much like a British links course in those high winds. We had to dig down 30 feet in the sand to build our own sandhills and the mechanical digger we used is enormous with wheels 6 feet in height. When the builders were shaping the course and settling the new landscape, there were fifty machines in action at one time. It is quite extraordinary that from a flat surface, the golf course was completed in eleven months – planted, mowed and playable.

On one golf course we were building in Naples, Florida, the project was held up for a full year because there was a pair of woodpeckers on the property of such a rare species that we had to change the routing plan of the course. The woodpeckers were the bosses. In fact they are responsible for some of the new design and I just hoped they would not decide to fly off to another hole. And in Houston, we were about to design a golf course when we discovered that there were a couple of wildcats on the island. So we had to come up with a plan to ensure they were undisturbed – and also that they presented no threat to golfers.

There are so many considerations involved in golf course design that people never imagine, quite apart from the more obvious fundamentals of remembering where the sun will be at certain times of the day and how it will affect players. As a general rule, it is not a good idea to oblige golfers to play into the setting sun – in other words, to design a west-facing final hole. But it does happen and is sometimes unavoidable. Then there is the civil engineering aspect of golf course creation. At Alaqua, for example we had to sink our drainage system in this thick, sticky, black, muddy soil – it looks like seafood gumbo – and it was a monumental task. Sometimes the land can be easy but more often than not it is tough. In Hawaii we were asked to build a golf course on literally millions and millions of chunks of lava, some of which were 8 feet tall. It was one mass of rock. So the primary process had to be to go in there and crush all this black lava and then reshape the landscape. A huge challenge but typical of the projects in unlikely places that constantly draw upon all my years of playing experience to incorporate and use in these different sites.

One of the precepts in my design work is that I build holes that will challenge me – in others words that I would like to play – but that also have the flexibility to accommodate the complete range of golfers. A championship tee for professionals, for example, can be placed some considerable distance back behind scrub and bush because there is no serious problem for such players to carry a ball 150 yards or more over that stuff. In turn, this cuts down on the maintenance costs of a championship tee because the only cost is for a little bit of irrigation. Maintenance considerations are very important in golf course design, with some courses needing millions of dollars a year to be kept in reasonable condition. That is why the golf courses in the British Isles are so far ahead because they have tackled maintenance so intelligently.

Part of the satisfaction I derive from golf course design is being able to transform what might appear to be a rather ordinary piece of land into a test that looks as though it has always been part of the landscape. For me, this work combines my love of the land with my love of golf, and in practical terms brings together artistry and economics.

There is no point in producing a masterpiece without any thought to its subsequent running costs. I played a course in Arizona on which a million gallons of water a day had to be pumped just to keep it playable in the relentless sunshine. Not only were the costs enormous but the effect on the local water level was quite severe. And there is a course in California which costs $2 million a year to maintain and which will become more expensive as the years pass. Thus the golf course designer must always balance his creativity with the bottom line in terms of costs. This is one of the reason why I am not a particular fan of the work of Robert Trent Jones. In fact, I do not know many professional golfers who are fans of his courses. His bunkering is too large and too extreme. The cost of maintaining huge bunkers is very high and even the size of these hazards – some of them 40-yard long monsters beside the green – suggest an attempt to bully the player instead of locating the exact spot at which to punish an errant shot.

There is, however, another consideration involved in modern golf course design. As golf equipment and skills improve with the years, is it good enough to withstand the test of time? Or will it become out of date and something of a relic? More importantly, what can be done to sustain its challenge? The truly great courses have already answered such doubts and questions. And this is certainly true of my short-list of favourite golf courses in the world. They have an enduring quality that owes nothing to fashion and I never grow tired of playing them.

My supreme favourite is Pine Valley in New Jersey. It has tremendous character and is a formidable foe. Basically, it is a collection of tees and greens and occasional islands of fairways set in sandy wasteland and pine forest. It has been called the toughest golf course in the world. It requires a kind of stepping-stone golf as well as pinpoint accuracy. Truly, it is the ultimate test.

For its scenic splendour and a unique completeness, Cypress Point on the rugged Californian coastline close to Pebble Beach and Monterey is also a favourite. It is the complete golf course because its terrain offers a hint of parkland which expands into a form of heathland and then a stretch of links by the sea, thus combining all forms of golf as we know it. It is a magical spot and contains one of golf's most famous holes – the short sixteenth where tee and green are perched either side of a cove above the raging Pacific Ocean. The brave man bids for the green knowing full well the penalties of failure. His cautious opponent settles for a mid-iron along the clifftop with the outside hope of a chip and a putt to save his par. It remains, therefore, the classic example of strategic golf – unlike Pine Valley which follows in the penal tradition of architecture because there are no safe options; no easy way to play the course.

My third choice must be Augusta National, and not simply because of the memories of victories it holds for me. Essentially Augusta – or rather, Bobby Jones and Alister Mackenzie who designed it – got golf's equation absolutely right in that the player is allowed a selection of strategies and is then rewarded or punished in proportion to the degree of skill displayed.

There is, however, a basic error in the concept of Augusta's greens. Their surface is extremely fast, which is an acceptable characteristic provided the greens are reasonably flat. The trouble with Augusta's greens is that they have been contoured so severely that the combination of speed and slope make them almost impossible to play. This may be partly due to modern technology. When Augusta's greens were constructed in the 1930s, the high-tech mowing equipment and fine-leafed bent brass did not exist. Their advent has given the decision-makers the opportunity to turn undulating greens on the older courses into monsters that are almost unplayable. I have putted off the green on the short twelfth hole on two occasions. I watched Tom Watson try to hole from 3 feet on the second green. He gave the ball the merest touch and missed the target then faced a return putt of 30 feet. Mark Hayes once had a 5-footer on the last green and then had a 50-footer coming back. That is ludicrous.

Arnold Palmer remains one of the foremost authorities on Augusta and one of its greatest admirers yet firmly believes the greens were never designed to accommodate the kind of bent grass that is now on them. In general terms, a green should have a drop of no more than 2 feet – a slope if you will – from its back to the front edge. At Augusta that difference is about 6 feet which, when the speed of the bent grass is taken into consideration, reduces putting to something between a lottery and a farce. Clearly the greens have been made too fast for the slopes and I think it has been done because players began to score so well that there was a fear by Augusta officials that their famous course might become a little obsolete. But what really is wrong with scores getting lower? Other sports are not afraid of these measurable improvements.

I know it can never be quite the same in golf. While the modern sprinter is still basically competing under the same sort of conditions Jesse Owens faced in the 1930s and therefore his running time is relevant, the modern golfer has greater advantages over his predecessors – better golf balls, clubs and finely manicured fairways and greens – so that comparisons are unsafe. What matters is that the integrity of the game is preserved and that the challenge of the golf course itself is fashioned to keep pace with these improving skills. How that is done remains the responsibility of each designer.

There is no obvious Player style in course design – except, I hope, the absence of the obvious weaknesses I have outlined and abhor. The challenge for me is that over the years I can give pleasure to thousands of people who will play my courses. I will have made a contribution and left evidence of my values and philosophies on the game. It is a thrilling thought.

CHAPTER 18
... and Onwards

Whatever the precise origins of the royal and ancient game which some historians suggest began along the Scottish seashores more than 500 years ago, its basic challenge has not changed in all that time. Many many generations of enthusiasts down the centuries have tackled the same objective of hitting a ball cross-country to demonstrate their dexterity, skill and judgement, quite apart from their strength of character when rivalry is involved.

That said, it is fair to say that for the last fifty years of its hitherto untroubled and constant existence, the game of golf has had to fight to preserve its character in the face of relentless developments in the playing qualities of both club and ball, as well as the astounding improvements in preparation and condition of the fields of play.

Any assessment of the game's future must therefore first study its past to identify obvious trends and changes that might offer some clue as to where the game is going; whether it remains on the right path or is drifting towards dangers that will rob it of its original and essential challenge.

Some traditionalists have argued against many of the new developments, insisting, for example, that the artificial watering of golf courses robs the game of its original arbitrary nature – those freak bounces and the constant need to judge how far the ball will run along the ground – while reducing the quality of the test itself to the docility of a dartboard.

They contend that the game – in its best form – was always meant to have an unpredictable element, the random breaks that were part of the original cross-country test, and that to attempt to iron out as many problems as possible is to rob the sport of this essential character.

The weakness of that proposition, if followed to its obvious conclusion, is that the sport of golf would never have moved from its seashore environment if only those conditions were to be maintained, because that was the natural terrain upon which it came into existence.

Yet the fact remains that the game did spread inland while attempting to maintain as much as possible of the character and form of the original, so that, for example, what we now regard as bunkers or sand traps were simply attempts to reproduce the natural sandy hollows among the hills and dunes.

One effect of bringing the game away from its original wide open habitat of the shoreline to the inland restrictions of pastures, meadows, heaths and parks was that the basic principle of 'hit it, find it and hit it again' could not be observed quite so fully because of the variety of complications to be found – fences, brooks, lakes, etc., etc. Consequently, the basic rules inevitably increased to cope with the volume of case law presented by the varying situations that occurred so that parity, never before considered a prime factor in the original game, suddenly became an essential condition. And here again the traditionalists argued that this process of trying to legislate unfairness out of the game, once embarked upon, could only mean that the size of the rule-book would grow *ad infinitum* as more and more incidents required clarification year after year and all the law-makers could do was try and slow that inevitable growth.

The development of the professional game as a form of public entertainment has also had its effect on the rules, in that special dispensations have to be accorded if only to observe the principle that the show must go on. At times, this can alter the fundamentals of the game.

For example, the obvious principle of medal play is that everybody should play exactly the same course, otherwise competition is meaningless. However, it is quite permissible and obviously expedient in a professional event to alter the course in order to keep the event in progress. If, during a storm, a green becomes waterlogged and the hole submerged during a round, then a new hole can be cut on unaffected ground. In strict terms, the same course has not therefore been played by the entire field, yet common sense demands this kind of option.

Then, too, there are the trimmings and trappings of tournament golf which at times literally come into play – the hospitality tents, advertising signs, television towers and miles of cables that flank almost every fairway. That ancient stick-and-ball game along the seashore could never have envisaged any such hazards. None of them form a natural aspect of the game and therefore all of them need special legislation.

But perhaps the greatest pressure on the character of the game in modern times has come from science itself and the astonishing advances and inventions which have enhanced – or perhaps reduced – the skill factor. This is where the greatest threat now lies and the legislators constantly scrutinize each new invention to see if it contravenes their rules.

The 'black museum' at the Royal and Ancient Golf Club of St Andrews, which jointly governs the game worldwide with the United States Golf Association, contains an armoury of bizarre clubs which were designed to make the game easier for the golfer but which have failed the test because they do not conform to the basic form and outline of a golf club.

Moreover, it is now possible to construct a golf ball that will fly great distances; but clearly such a characteristic would undermine the yardage value of every golf course which in turn would mean that par would also lose meaning because it would be quite impossible for every golf course in the world to extend its length to cope with the performance of the longer flying ball.

Consequently the law-makers felt obliged to impose a speed limit on the golf ball – a velocity rate which cannot exceed 250 feet per second as the ball leaves the clubhead. This is a classic example of the rules of golf being compelled to catch up with and contain scientific ingenuity and invention, which otherwise could transform a game that was played originally with shaped sticks and a leather ball filled with swan feathers.

In such terms the law-makers see their role as preserving the integrity of the game primarily by maintaining its fundamental character. Thus when some golfers found the business of putting became easier if they adopted a croquet-style action, hitting from behind and standing across the line of play, the law-makers felt this contravened the essential sideways hitting action that had always been part of golf and the swing itself. The method was outlawed, much to the chagrin of senior players who found the style to be a superb cure for the putting twitch.

When a manufacturer devised a golf ball that seemed to be self-correcting because of its weight distribution, once again the law-makers felt compelled to rule against it because they regarded it as an artificial aid likely to help a player with his or her stroke-making. Where is the sanction in a poorly executed stroke that should have resulted in a hook or a slice and possibly an awaiting hazard, if the ball rights itself and travels straight?

This particular battle was actually fought out in a court of law in the United States before the matter was resolved, but it offered evidence of the pressures being put on the game by scientific advance and the seriousness with which the law-makers felt they had to defend it.

There is, however, a school of thought which suggests that any development which improves performance and skill should be welcomed and that, just as better standards in other sports are gauged by faster times, higher or longer jumps, etc., so golf itself should not be frightened of lower scores – say in the 50s – but rather should enthusiastically accept the defined improvement.

And yet a delicate balance has to be struck between an acceptance of better standards that are based on improved skills and those developments that are seen to be caused primarily by special equipment which makes the task easier. This was the core of the argument over the size and shape of grooves cut in the face of certain makes of iron clubs, in that such clubs, even in the less skilled hands, were seen to improve performance in terms of accuracy and control. In short, they imparted considerable backspin on the ball particularly from the rough and as, by inference, the man playing from the rough is clearly less accurate than and therefore inferior to a player who keeps the ball in the fairway, the game seemed to be losing the sanction between rough and fairway. Moreover, the margin between the good player who never missed a fairway and his erratic rival had narrowed by virtue of the playing characteristics of these clubs which offered safe deliverance from the rough.

I can remember the time when it took massive skill to play over a trap and stop the ball close to the pin. It took great skill and the better players had an obvious and rightful advantage. But with the square clubface grooves, as well as a variety of new club shafts and particular types of golf ball, the average and poorer golfers are closing the gap.

It means the man with the greater talent is being affected. Even the metal-headed woods are having their effect on playing standards because they make the game easier for players in that they can get the golf ball airborne very easily.

That said, I accept that progress and development are inevitable and cannot be obstructed. I accept that the game must change to survive, just as it moved in the distant past from the feathery to the gutta-percha ball to the rubber-cored ball and from hickory shafts to steel and other refinements, including aluminium, fibreglass and carbon fibre. But above all, the integrity of the sport must be maintained and the skill factor preserved.

Of course, some have argued that perhaps the answer to all weird and wonderful inventions and the inherent dangers of inconsistency they pose would be to produce a standard issue of club and ball for all players when they compete in championships, so that everybody started on an even basis and true skills could be compared.

The apparent reason for this view is that the wide range of golf balls now used in tournaments demonstrates such vastly differing characteristics from high flight to low trajectory as to make fair comparison invalid. Moreover, so the argument goes, the variety of individually tailored clubs, many of them acquired over years of trial and error, means that totally different strategies are at work in producing good scores.

But why not? I see such diversification as a strength of golf. There is no single right way to produce a good score. It is left to an individual's ingenuity and skill to devise the best possible method on the day.

I have other objections to this idea of a standard club and ball, because they still would not achieve the parity they pursue. Let's assume we all have the same equipment, right? One man plays in the morning when the wind is at its height and another plays in the afternoon when the wind has died. Parity has gone out of the window and the difference in scores will prove it.

Furthermore, I think in manufacturing terms such an idea would ruin free enterprise; and in any case golf itself is a game of judgement and that must include being able to choose what is considered to be the right equipment for the job.

I remember how puzzled some observers were during the 1974 British Open at Royal Lytham St Annes when I relied heavily on a one iron from a number of tees instead of a driver or fairway wood. Quite simply, my judgement insisted it was more important to keep the ball in play irrespective of what marginal distance might be lost from the tee.

It was my choice. I had selected my instruments to suit my strategy and I do not think such an option should be removed from the game. The game cannot be held back, particularly when professional golfers have devoted their lives to taking it towards new peaks of achievement.

The note-book is a case in point. There was a time when 'seeing' the shot that was about to be played was judged to be an essential skill as a golfer not only assessed by eye how far he had to play but also sensed what kind of shot was needed – high, low, hook or fade. All that changed, however, when the professionals began to take measurements of each hole, spotting their own landmarks so that at all times they knew exactly what distance had to be covered. It was an obvious part of an equation which had begun on the practice ground where they hit each club with such precise repetition that its range was known to the yard.

While clearly golfers have always made mental notes about distances and landmarks, the full-scale chart is a late development which has been credited to Deane Beman, the US Tour Commissioner, who started the practice in his playing days and saw it adopted later by Jack Nicklaus.

It is of course now standard procedure with tournament professionals, many of whom build up dossiers on championship courses they have played over the years. I remember during a practice round at Royal Lytham in 1974, Jack Nicklaus remarked that a telegraph pole had been removed from the road adjacent to one of the outward holes. He was looking at his notes for the 1963 championship there and had spotted the difference.

One of the more obvious reasons for the practice of note-taking is that globe-trotting professionals simply do not have time to get to know each course fully; to acquire the local knowledge of its character and mood. In times past, golfers might have made two or three visits to a championship venue in the months previous to the event, but the demands of the modern tournament schedule make that idea impossible; so the note-book, with its charts of every hole containing landmarks and precise distances to the green, has become an essential method of instant knowledge. And not only for the tournament player. Most golf clubs now produce such charts for their visitors to enable them to play with confidence and to give them an idea of the distances involved.

Has the note-book robbed the game of some of its skill? Has it reduced club selection to a mathematical calculation? Perhaps, but the stroke still has to be executed properly. More to the point, in every other sport it is essential to be as fully prepared as possible so that anything less than this state of readiness is regarded, rightfully, as unforgivable sloppiness.

This, then, is the state of the game as I see it today. It has never been more popular. It attracts millions of people all over the world and has created a huge demand in golf course construction that reflects a growth rate unparalleled in any other sport.

In Japan, for example, the game has boomed in astounding fashion with upwards of 14.2 million golfers using 1,703 golf courses and 593 driving ranges in a relatively short period of time. Furthermore, there are 1,120 courses in the planning stage and another 400 under construction. That is the power of golf.

Its enduring attractions are manifold and extend far beyond the athletic skills involved. There is the perpetual battle of self-discipline, the test of character in adversity that demands unwavering integrity and promotes enduring friendship between rivals. It is a game in which the manner of playing matters more than the standard achieved. Indeed, the rule-book itself devotes its opening pages to the etiquette of the game.

There is, too, the 'good life' image to golf – the hallmark of an affluent society – though it is also true that golf exists in all forms, from the exclusivity of Augusta National, to the rollered desert of Colesberg, even to the fairways that weave a route between disused missile launchers on a British air base. It is still the same great game, attracts the same devotion and zeal. That is its strength.

I see no reason for it to change. The game has a great future because it is built on discipline and integrity and therefore is not in danger of being undermined. It is true, however, that the professional sport – and tournament stars in particular – now probably exert the greatest influence on the mass of its followers.

The tournament game remains the shop-window of the sport and with the proliferation of events all over the world, there has been a sustained attempt to give some tournaments more status – to lift them above the rest – although not quite alongside the four major championships: the US Masters, US Open, US PGA and British Open. History and precedent decree that these four events are the ultimate four classics of world golf. The value has been set and I see no compelling argument or force that will change that value. Nor does anybody else – once they have won one of these rare titles.

That said, the winning of a championship does not automatically give the title-holder the status of a champion in the true sense of the word. It is a fact that in recent times the roll call of winners in the majors has often included candidates whose greatest claim was to have been in the right place at the right time and who probably will not feature often – if ever – again as champions. This has led to criticisms of complacency and laziness, particularly in American golf which still seeks a homegrown hero to follow in the footsteps of Arnold Palmer, Jack Nicklaus, Lee Trevino and Tom Watson. One argument is that there is too much prize money around now so that winning is no longer important because it is possible to make a handsome living each week without always going through the pressure of trying to win.

This, I feel, belies the competitive instinct which I believe motivates every professional to a greater or lesser extent. The game is about winning, not about making a weekly pay cheque. I think a softness of spirit may well have crept into the game; but it is not immediately connected with money. My view is that the all-exempt tour is a more likely cause of the loss of competitive edge that has occurred on the American tour and has led to various signs of international decline, including a succession of Ryder Cup failures against the best European professionals.

I think the system which guarantees the full complement of US Tour players a place in every event they choose to enter once they have qualified for the season must lead to weakening of intent, which in turn diminishes the will to win. In times past, the week-to-week pre-qualifying system in which many players had to earn their place, while tough, kept players on their toes and bred a fierce competitive determination. And it is significant that the leading players in the world today – Greg Norman, Nick Faldo, Seve Ballesteros, Ian Woosnam, and others – went through that system in their formative years.

In any case, I refuse to bemoan the lack of superstars. I choose to regard golf today as being in a period of transition, when a new world order is being established; when the international stars make their presence felt as the game expands through every continent. In short, the giants of the game will emerge again just as they have done in the past and they will become the targets at which others aim as they themselves lift the game to new heights.

It might seem to follow that with a truly international flavour to the game at the very top, there would be a serious case for a Grand Prix of golf after the fashion of tennis and motor racing, in which the elite compete against each other all over the world. I am not sure, however, that the players think this idea will work.

They are committed to their own national circuits and in any case make international forays into the major championships and classic events all around the world. Without doubt, a Grand Prix of golf would determine beyond question who is the best player in the world; but that objective might not be enough to take the best golfers away on a globe-trotting tour.

What I dislike is the closed-shop policy that seems to operate at times between major circuits – mainly the US and European tours – and I would like to see players who have excelled, irrespective of their nationalities, being able to play ten tournaments in any country.

It is a fact that if a player has proved himself to be a box-office attraction then the sponsors and the public have a right to see him in action in whatever country he is invited to play, and it is not the business of the professionals in that country to keep him out. That cannot help the game. A man who has won a major championship should be allowed to play wherever he is invited. But for the rest, there is a perfectly valid entry system on both the Regular and Senior Tours that is open to everybody through the qualifying schools in which they can prove they are good enough.

My judgement of a golfer, anyway, rests on the number and quality of the tournaments he has won and not the amount of cash he has amassed. In fact, cash would be the last of the criteria I would use. David Frost, my fellow countryman, won $2 million in two tournaments, which is more than I earned in my entire career on the US Regular Tour – which, among other wins, included nine major titles.

It is also my considered view that the present-day golfers are no better than their famous predecessors of, say, fifty years ago, and that Byron Nelson, Ben Hogan and Sam Snead, given the equipment, prize money, conditions of golf courses and convenience of travel that now exist, still would have been world-beaters. I happen to believe that the special fire that burns within a man will make him a champion whatever his generation. I say that because I recognize it in the venerable Gene Sarazen as much as I see it in the succeeding generations epitomized by Seve Ballesteros and Nick Faldo. That too, offers hope for the future of the game.

I suppose I am no different from any other golfer who cares about the game when it comes to aspects of it that I would like to see changed or refined. We all have pet bees in our bonnets. I think, for example, that there are far too many rules and that there should be a determined effort to reduce the number. As a first step, it might be possible to simplify and reduce some of the penalties. Take, for example, the stroke and distance penalty for a lost ball. It is a harsh sanction and out of proportion to the error involved. Consider this case: you hit a drive 300 yards and the ball trickles out of bounds by an inch. That means you have earned a stroke and distance penalty and are playing your third from the tee.

But say, instead of connecting for a 300-yard drive, you miss the ball completely, which must be an infinitely worse mistake. Now, however, you count only the stroke that missed and are playing only two from the tee. There is a glaring inconsistency in such penalties. Two errors from the same spot – but differing punishments.

I would like to see a determined return towards a basic principle of law, in that the ball must be played as it lies, so that players do not find themselves getting relief from all manner of objects. It seems to happen too often on golf courses and many times evades or at least minimizes the deserved penalty of a poor shot.

I think, too, that slow play has become the curse of the game and has permeated from the top of the sport right down to club level. It ought to be safe enough to assume that players are ready to hit when it is their turn to play and that there is no need for the snail-pace deliberations, throwing grass in the air to test wind strength and direction, that have become an integral part of the golf swing of some professionals.

Sadly, such antics are copied so that golf courses all over the world find themselves clogged by enthusiasts who perceive slow golf to be good golf. Not so. Though various fines have been imposed at times on notorious slowcoaches on both sides of the Atlantic in tournaments and officials have even laid down specific times for fairway shots, putts etc., the ultimate penalty is threatened but never used.

If an offending player had a two-stroke penalty slapped on him for slow play and he were later to lose the tournament as a result, the sanction would have served its purpose, robbing him not only of a title but of a hefty cash prize which would amount to a hefty fine. It would be a bad moment but must remain the ultimate punishment for those who constantly offend and disregard procedures, setting a bad example to others.

All my life I have seen golf as a giant brotherhood, from the days when I was a junior member in Johannesburg to these times when I am a regular campaigner on the Seniors Tour. I suppose there is a missionary zeal about me when it comes to spreading the word about golf because I realize how much it has to offer.

I want as many people as possible to get involved, to enjoy it and benefit from it. This is one of the reasons I am establishing Gary Player golf academies worldwide where youngsters and even adult beginners can learn to play the game according to my philosophies. It is good news and I want to share it.

During the 1990 Million Dollar Challenge at Sun City, young Tommy Armour III, the grandson of the great Scottish champion, implored me to give him a lesson on how to play bunker shots. I readily agreed and soon had him hitting recovery shots with great confidence. It occurred to me afterwards that in less than 40 minutes I had passed on to Tommy secrets and techniques that had taken me a lifetime to learn. But no matter. That too is the joy of golf; an ability to put somebody in need on the right path. Such knowledge is certainly not meant to be kept hidden. Therein, too, lies a Christian message which makes me happy.

In truth, probably the greatest contribution any man can make is by his example. If now, or at some time in the future, somebody draws strength from this personal story of the lonely, undersized boy from South Africa who refused to accept the odds both on and off the fairways and triumphed against them, then my purpose has been served. It was all worthwhile. There will remain some memory that I had striven to be the best. And that I refused to settle for less.

Appendix

Gary Player US Tour Career Earnings and Year-by-Year Position

Year	Position	Earnings
1957	–	$3,286
1958	–	$18,591
1959	58	$5,694
1960	28	$13,879
1961	1	$64,540
1962	6	$45,838
1963	5	$55,455
1964	7	$61,449
1965	5	$69,964
1966	38	$26,391
1967	18	$55,820
1968	33	$51,950
1969	5	$123,897
1970	15	$101,212
1971	5	$120,916
1972	7	$120,719
1973	63	$48,878
1974	19	$108,372
1975	27	$73,943
1976	53	$53,668
1977	21	$112,485
1978	9	$177,336
1979	53	$74,482
1980	76	$45,471
1981	122	$22,483
1982	145	$22,059
1983	147	$20,567
1984	70	$93,258
1985	175	$11,032
		total $1,795,994

Gary Player US Seniors Tour Earnings and Year-by-Year Position

Year	Position	Earnings
1985	44	$30,000
1986	5	$291,190
1987	6	$333,439
1988	2	$435,914
1989	4	$514,116
1990	9	$507,268
		total **$2,111,927**

The Dominant Years of the 'Big Three'

Year	US Masters	US Open	British Open	US PGA
1959	–	–	**Player**	–
1960	Palmer	Palmer	–	–
1961	**Player**	–	Palmer	–
1962	Palmer	Nicklaus	Palmer	**Player**
1963	Nicklaus	–	–	Nicklaus
1964	Palmer	–	–	–
1965	Nicklaus	**Player**	–	–
1966	Nicklaus	–	Nicklaus	–
1967	–	Nicklaus	–	–
1968	–	–	**Player**	–
1969	–	–	–	–
1970	–	–	Nicklaus	–
1971	–	–	–	Nicklaus
1972	Nicklaus	Nicklaus	–	**Player**
1973	–	–	–	Nicklaus
1974	**Player**	–	**Player**	–
1975	–	–	–	–
1976	–	–	–	–
1977	–	–	–	–
1978	**Player**	–	Nicklaus	–

Gary Player in the Majors – Top 10 Finishes

Year	US Masters	US Open	British Open	US PGA
1958	–	2	–	–
1959	–	–	1	–
1960	6	–	8	–
1961	1	9	–	–
1962	2	4	–	1
1963	4	8	7	–
1964	4	–	8	–
1965	2	1	–	–
1966	–	–	4	3
1967	6	–	3	–
1968	7	–	1	–
1969	–	–	–	2
1970	3	–	–	–
1971	6	–	7	–
1972	10	–	6	1
1973	–	–	–	–
1974	1	8	7	1
1975	–	–	–	–
1976	–	–	–	–
1977	–	10	–	–
1978	1	6	–	–
1979	–	2	–	–
1980	6	–	–	–
1981	–	–	–	–
1982	–	–	–	–
1983	–	–	–	–
1984	–	–	–	–

Gary Player in the Seniors

Year	US Open	British Open	US PGA
1985	–	–	–
1986	2	3	1
1987	1	7	8
1988	1	1	1
1989	9	–	8
1990	3	1	1

Gary Player Notable Wins

1955
East Rand Open
Egyptian Matchplay
South African PGA Challenge

1956
East Rand Open
South African Open
Dunlop Tournament
Ampol

1957
Australian PGA
Coughs Harbour
Transvaal Open

1958
Natal Open
Kentucky Derby
Australian Open
Ampol
Coughs Harbour

1959
Transvaal Open
South African PGA
Natal Open
Western Province Open
Dunlop Masters
British Open
Victoria Open

1960
South African Open
South African PGA
Dunlop Masters
Transvaal Open
Natal Open
Western Province Open

1961
US Masters
Lucky International Open
Sunshine Open
Yomiuri Open
Ampol

1962
Transvaal Open
Natal Open
US PGA Championship
Australian Open

1963
Sponsored 5000
Transvaal Open
Liquid Air
Richelieu Grand Prix Capetown
Richelieu Grand Prix
    Johannesburg
Dunlop Masters
San Diego Open
Australian Open

1964
Dunlop Masters
Pensacola Open
500 Festival Open

1965
South African Open
US Open
World Series
World Matchplay
NTL Challenge Cup
World Cup Individual
Australian Open

1966
South African Open
Natal Open
Transvaal Open
World Matchplay

1967
Dunlop Masters
South African Open

1968
South African Open
Natal Open
Western Province Open
World Series
British Open
World Matchplay
Australian Wills Masters

1969
South African Open
South African PGA
Tournament of Champions
Australian Open
Australian Wills Masters

1970
Greater Greensboro Open
Australian Open
Dunlop International

1971
General Motors
Western Province Open
Dunlop Masters
Jacksonville Open
National Airlines Open
World Matchplay

1972
Dunlop Masters
South African Open
Western Province Open
Dunlop Masters

US PGA
World Series
New Orleans Open
Japan Airlines Open
Brazilian Open

1973
General Motors Open
Southern Open
World Matchplay

1974
Dunlop Masters
Rand International
General Motors
US Masters
Memphis Classic
British Open
Ibergolf Tournament
La Manag Tournament
Australian Open
Brazilian Open

1975
South African Open
General Motors Classic
Lancôme Trophy

1976
Dunlop Masters
South African Open
Dunlop Masters
General Motors Open

1977
South African Open
ICL Transvaal
World Cup Individual

1978
USA Masters
Tournament of Champions
Houston Classic

1979
South African Open
South African PGA
Kronenbräu Masters
Sun City

1980
Trophée Boigny
Chilean Open

1981
South African PGA

1983
US Skins Game

1984
Johnnie Walker Trophy

1985
Quadel Seniors Classic

1986
PGA Seniors Championship
United Hospitals Senior
   Championship
Denver Post Champions of Golf

1987
Mazada Seniors TPC
Northville Invitational
USGA Seniors
World Series Invitational
Nissan Skins Game

1988
US PGA Seniors Championship
Aetna Challenge
Southwestern Bell Classic
USGA Seniors
GTE North Classic
British Seniors Open
Nissan Skins Game

1989
GTE North Classic
RJR Championship
Nissan Skins Game

1990
US PGA Seniors Championship
British Seniors Championship

1991
Key Biscane Seniors . . .

Golf Courses Designed by Gary Player

Completed Courses

USA

Royal Oaks Golf Club, Cartersville, Georgia
Berkeley Hills Country Club, Norcross, Georgia
Pine Isle Country Club, Lake Lanier, Georgia
Bent Creek Mountain Inn Country Club, Gatlingburg, Tenessee
Cartersville Country Club, Georgia
River North Golf and Country Club, Macon, Georgia
Dolphin Head Golf Club, Hilton Head Island, South Carolina
Alto Lakes Golf and Country Club, New Mexico
Marsh Point Golf Club, Kiawah Island, South Carolina
Brander Mill Country Club, Midlothian, Virginia
North River Golf Club, Tuscalousa, Alabama
Fair Oaks Ranch Golf and Country Club, Boerne, Texas (now
     remodelling)
Hilton Head National, Hilton Head Island, South Carolina
Standard Club, Atlanta, Georgia
Pacific Golf Club, San Clemente, California
Hilton Head Plantation, Hilton Head Island, South Carolina
Laurel Oak, Sarasota, Florida
Cypress Knoll, Palm Coast, Florida
Steele Canyon, El Cajon, California
River Run Golf Club, Ocean City, Maryland
River Falls Plantation, Spartanburg, South Carolina
White Cliffs of Plymouth, Plymouth, Massachusetts
Alaqua Country Club, Longwood, Florida
Nob North Golf Club, Dalton, Georgia*
Hogan Park, Midland, Texas*
Shawnee Municipal Institute, West Virginia*
Pebble Brook Country Club, Manchester, Georgia*
Warner Robins, AFB, Golf Club, Georgia*
Pole Creek Golf Club, Tabernash, Colorado*
Alpine Valley Golf Club, Crete, Illinois*
Twin Valley Country Club, Wadesboro, North Carolina*
Oak Hills Country Club, San Antonio, Texas*
Midland Country Club, Texas*

*Golf courses designed with Kirby, Player and Associates

Puerto Rico

Palmas del Mar Golf Club, Humacao

Europe

Almerimar Golf Club, El Ejido, Almeria, Spain
El Paradiso Golf Club, Estepona, Malaga, Spain
Escorpion Golf Club, Betera, Valencia, Spain
Mas Palomas, Mas Palomas, Spain
The Edinburgh Course, Wentworth, UK
Maspalomas Golf Course, Canary Islands

Japan

Odawara Golf Club
Mikasayama, Nara
Kumamoto, Kyushu
Miigata Forest Golf Club, Toyoura Village*
Nishi Nihon Golf Club, Nogata*
Odawara Getenloa, Gothenba*

Philippines

Lake Pasay Golf Club, Iloocos Norte*
Wack Wack Golf and Country Club, Manila*
Puerto Azul Golf Club, Pasay City*
Kamirag Golf Club, Cebu Island*

Africa

Riviera Africaine Golf Club, Abidjan, Ivory Coast

South Africa

Gary Player Country Club, Sun City, Bophuthatswana
Roodeport Country Club, Johannesburg
Crown Mines Golf Club, Johannesburg
Kensington Golf Club, Johannesburg*
Lenasia CountryClub, Johannesburg
Fish River Sun Golf Club, Ciskei
Flamingo Lake Golf Club, Welkom
Fancourt Country Club, George
Dainfern Country Club, Fourways, JHB

Courses Under Design or Construction

USA

The Classics, Naples, Florida
Country Side Country Club, Clearwater, Florida
The Fountains, St Augustine, Florida
Alaqua Lakes, Longwood, Florida
Geneva National, Lake Geneva, Wisconsin
Sebago Lake Resort, Casco, Maine
Lyman Meadows, Wallingford, Connecticut
Pinewild (No. 9), Pinehurst, South Carolina
City of West Palm Beach, Florida
Country Club of New Jersey
Tapawingo Country Club, St Louis
Jacumba Valley, California
Lake Las Vegas, Henderson, New York
Country Club of New York, Rockland, New York
Indianapolis, Mann Corp, Minnesota
Mission Hills, Palm Springs, California
Lely Resort, Naples, Florida
Jacumba Valley, Jacumba, California

Canada

Royal Shediak, New Brunswick

Puerto Rico

Costa Isabella

Europe

Château de Taulane, Taulane, France
Five Nations Country Club, Méan, Belgium
St Anna, Cagolesso, Italy
Tuscany Cavalieri, Sienna, Italy
Bad Munder Golf Park, Hanover, Germany

Israel

Eilat Golf Course, Eilat

Australia
Tanglewood Valley, New South Wales

Japan
Matsuzaki, Izu Peninsula

Philippines
Lian Basangas

Taiwan
Pao Fu Golf and Country Club, Kwan Si
Pei Pin Country Club, Linkou

Malaysia
Desaru, Johore

Thailand
Sriracha International, Changwat, Cholburi

South Africa
Malane, Transvaal
Secunda, Transvaal
Peach Tree Country Club, Transvaal
Kruger Park Lodge, Eastern Transvaal

Other Achievements

1966: Bobby Jones Award from USGA, for Distinguished
    Sportsmanship in Golf
Leading money winner of the PGA tour in 1961
Inducted into the World Golf Hall of Fame in 1974
In 1990 was awarded Sportsman of the Century in South Africa
Shot a record 59 when he won the Brazilian Open in 1973

Victory Records

Has won over 150 events worldwide and is recognized as the
International Ambassador of Golf. Fifth on the most Senior PGA
Tour Victory Records winning 21 Senior Tour events internationally

Miscellaneous Records

He has been Top 10 on the Money List for the last five years in a row
    on the Senior Tour.
Last man to win three tournaments in a row on the US PGA Tour, in
    1978 winning the Masters.

Index